A
WATCHER IN THE
WOODS

A
WATCHER IN THE
WOODS

Patricia Sibley

WHITTET BOOKS

First published 1990
Text © 1990 by Patricia Sibley
Illustrations © 1990 by Lyn O'Neill

Whittet Books Ltd, 18 Anley Road, London W14 0BY

Design by Paul Saunders

British Library Cataloguing in Publication Data

Sibley, P.
    A watcher in the woods
    1. Deer
    II. Title
    599.7357

    ISBN 0-905483-82-0

Typeset by Litho Link Ltd, Welshpool, Powys, Wales
Printed and bound by
Bookcraft (Bath) Ltd.

For
ELIZABETH RUTTER
Dear Liz whose hospitality
made much of my watching
possible

ACKNOWLEDGMENTS

My grateful thanks to Steve Smith, Robin Fletcher, Barbara Wakeford, John Buck, Les Barber and various members of the Forestry Commission who prefer to have their whereabouts unknown.

CONTENTS

INTRODUCTION

Years ago, while on another writing assignment in the country, I fell in love with fallow deer and determined to write a book about them. Yet when I reached their woods the fallow had often vanished away and instead there would be a perky little roe, a sika stag black from wallowing or a whole herd of red deer – and who could be disappointed? So my scope was widened to include any kind of deer who crossed my path. But then, who could ignore a badger eating jam sandwiches by moonlight or a pair of fox cubs out human-watching?

So while this book is mainly about deer watching, there are many intruders, both furred and feathered. I have watched from Mull to the New Forest, on heathland and lakeside, in ancient woodlands and new plantations, but for the sake of the deer who must always come first, the exact locations remain secret. Buckland Water is a real river but not to be traced on any mundane map. I owe many wonderful deer-hours to friends and keepers who have honoured me with their confidence.

The sections were planned to include as wide a variety of countryside as possible and originally each was to be devoted to a different kind of deer, Kings Ash to fallow, but then the red deer moved in, Fenny Cross to sika, but the bucks had fled away . . . so here are reflected many of those chance encounters which bring such delight to any watcher in the woods.

Patricia Sibley
February 1990

KINGS ASH

THREE piebald donkeys stood motionless in the middle of the narrow forest road, holding up traffic, sedate and sober like elderly ladies disapproving of the twentieth century and therefore ignoring it, but eventually I edged past and soon came to Kings Ash, the stretch of forest that I love best, to look for red deer.

A windless November day, pale sun netting the wood with twig shadows, great oaks and beeches spreading away wide-spaced down the northern slope; the wild country enveloped me, a magic land full of secrets, though the October storms had torn down most of the leaves so you could see far into the wood across the fox-coloured floor. In the thin sunlight, beech boles gleamed pewter-grey, their northern flanks dark with moss, spreading up from the long sinews of root. A nuthatch tap-tapped high among the bare branches; an acorn fell with a loud splat; a single sweet chestnut leaf, a glowing amber, dropped slowly through the air turning over and over; otherwise all was still. Chestnut leaves are beautiful, but a hazard, as they crisp and rustle underfoot stiff as paper. Fortunately we were still some way from the herd's afternoon resting place. November is one of the few times when a mixed herd of stags, hinds and young ones can be seen together; usually red deer split up along sex lines. They had congregated for the fever of the autumn rut: now, with all that excitement over, the stags would very soon drift away to form their own groups. Later each would mooch off alone for the private ritual of antler dropping (an annual event).

For the last five years of watching in the woods, my companion has been George, a black-and-tan, long-haired dachshund, tireless, gay, totally devoted to me but of uncertain temper to others. He walks courteously past all forest creatures without so much as a glance – except for grey squirrels. Those he is allowed to chase though I trust he never will catch one: not only am I concerned for the squirrels (of any colour), but I fear the effects of their long, sharp claws. Of course for close deer watching George has to be left behind; on this occasion I was expecting only a distant view.

Nearing the wood's edge, I sat down on a fallen oak and George at once came rollicking across the forest floor, stirring up tawny leaves so the air smelled earthy and bitter (sit down equals picnic). Leashed together we moved quietly westward to a natural viewpoint. The wood is an old enclosure, its boundary a mossy, broken bank some three feet above the level of the land beyond, a stretch of flat, marshy heath, the woods on the far side bordered by

thickets of rhododendrons. In their thick, all-season shelter, the red deer often lie up for the afternoon to chew the cud – or ruminate, a pleasanter word with its double meaning: at such times they do appear to be lost in thought.

Pause. Listen. Nearby only a blackbird scuttering about in some dead bracken with maximum fuss as usual, but up ahead, out beyond the trees, a glimpse of reddish brown colour, moving . . . then another, and another. Why, the whole herd must be there and grazing right over this side! Move slowly, carefully from tree bole to tree bole, hot with excitement in the chill air. Reach the bank, climb silently up behind the last oak and peer cautiously out from behind it, brown woolly hat pulled well down over eyebrows.

Marshy grass had already turned winter-sallow, patched with rusty bracken and the dead brown of old heather bushes. Out on the wetter ground, among clumps of rushes, lapwings were feeding, sometimes wheeling up and throwing themselves about the air in their curious abandoned way on blunt black wings, calling 'pee-wit, pee-wit'. Out across the heath, leathery rhododendron leaves shone dark green above bare spikes of bog myrtle. Beyond, a larch spinney kept some of its needles and glowed like a tapestry of gentle autumn ambers, yellows and browns. In all the wide peaceful spaces of the forest not a deer to be seen, only, close at hand and oblivious of me, three ponies, shaggy red-brown, cropped the better grass with a small tearing sound.

I should have remembered that red deer are not really red in winter, merely brown. Maybe they were here a minute ago, and had just faded away into those far woods; elusiveness is part of their character, part of the spell they cast upon me years ago when I first

12

began to write about the forest. One September morning, very early, I had woken and looked out of the cottage window. A slim young fallow buck was just stepping silently out of the surrounding copse into the orchard, and there he stood, dappled and brave, antlers gilded by the sun's early rays, the very spirit of the forest. (Never mind that he was after the Cox's Orange!) Fallow will always be my first love with their elegant lines and high-strung nerves. It was through them that I came to appreciate sika, red and roe, which also roam this wilderness.

Now the sun sank behind tall beeches on the rise and the world turned grey. Mist would rise soon, out on the marsh. We turned back into the woods: time yet still to find the herd. We would try on the southern side of the road this time. There is no room for disappointment in deer watching, only the hope of 'next time'. After all, red deer are the scarcest of all the breeds here, with only some fifty or sixty roaming the whole vast forest. In the quiet a robin tried out his wistful winter trill and away to the west, a tawny owl's cry shivers out 'hoo-hoo-hoooo' over Ferny Heath.

By the road, two Rottweilers had just leapt from a car and raced off southward along the path I had meant to take. They may have been dogs with lovely natures, but a mere whiff of them would send any deer leaping for cover, while the strident call of their lady owner in good tweeds shouting, 'Heel, Laurel, heel, Hardy,' (to no effect at all) would scatter birds from their roosts. Apart from all this disturbance, George would have felt it his duty to clear the place of Rottweiler, a breed he particularly dislikes, so there was no choice but to turn back into the northern woods for the last of the precious November daylight.

It is not possible to walk Kings Ash in a temper. Wordsworth said, 'There is a spirit in the woods,' and it is in the twilight one feels that presence most deeply. Every small rustle is part of a greater mystery. Circling round through wide-spaced oak and beech, I glimpsed a tiny movement ahead and stopped to look through binoculars. Several winters ago, winter gales had brought down one of these huge pollarded oaks. The branches were cut and carted away, but the great prone trunk was left as a home for wood mice, beetles and fungi. A lesser spotted woodpecker was working it over, not in the drumming frenzy of spring, but with patient probings of his long beak into every crevice in the deeply wrinkled bark. Some had come away from the trunk, hanging loose like an old coat: underneath would be a rich larder of woodlice and beetles. This little woodpecker, not much bigger than a sparrow, is quite rare here, so it was a treat to stand and admire the black wings smartly barred with white, and neat red cap, a tiny spot of colour in the grey air, revealing that this was a male. Now and then he stretched upright, staring round with quick turns of the head, but not sensing any danger, bounced along the trunk to attack another part, tossing bits of bark over his shoulder when they got in the way. He wore the stripe of dark feather at the base of the beak that gives every member of the woodpecker family a peculiarly sardonic expression, though it is most marked in the green.

Time to circle back to the road. George races on ahead, crashing through drifts of dead leaves. Trees are grey presences in the misty, dimming spaces of the wood. Suddenly George reappears, running back to me at full stretch, eyes rolling, a whimper in his throat, and throws himself at my knees. When I pick him up he is trembling from nose to tail, shoves a cold nose into my neck for comfort as he did when a frightened puppy.

Cautiously, I move on, following a track made by forestry lorries years ago, and now two parallel dips and ridges green with moss. Rounding an oak I come straight upon a red stag. He had been grazing on the moss, but raises his head at sight of me, though his jaws continue munching. He is young, with only three tines to each antler, but he still towers over me. (Tines, points or side branches, increase with each new set of antlers, so a stag in his prime might be a twelve pointer.) We stare at each other for what seems a long time, then, miraculously, treating me as just one more forest creature, he lowers his head, and begins to graze again. Leaning against the oak to break my outline, I become aware of small rustles all around in the dusky wood, and, peering about, see big dark shapes moving ponderously near, or standing still: eight, nine, ten. By one of those wonderful forest chances, the herd has come to me.

I shoved George under my coat (fortunately he is a miniature). The stag eyed me again then ambled a few steps westward. Three slightly smaller deer materialized out of the twilight; they were hinds, closely followed by a little gang of half-grown calves, each pausing for a mouthful of moss before moving slowly on, treading heavily through the leaf carpet. I realized the whole herd was on the move, westward, and I was in the very centre of them. A hind on her own stopped to stare at me with her big, dark, almond-shaped eyes, but the young ones behind hustled her on, two young stags, the only ones in a hurry. The rest moved by, ponderously, leaving an indefinable rich warm animal reek behind. Others wandered past out of sight behind me, but I heard big bodies blundering by, cracking twigs, lazily confident, without an enemy in the world.

Last of all, I thought, came the king stag. It was still just light enough to make out his underparts stained black from the last mud-wallow, a thick mane over the shaggy coat and magnificent antlers, many-tined, held proudly high as he marched past. Slowly the herd noise died away to our right. I was just about to break the spell, emerge from a world of deer, when twigs rustled to the left and a last stag appeared. He was very old, very thin, his antlers tall but spindly, his muzzle grey down the middle, but he ambled gamely off after the herd.

A muffled snort under my coat recalled me to the world. Cramped and cold, I made for the road but could not resist a final look westward. A small night wind had sneaked up from the south-west, creaking bare branches together, skittering among old leaves. As I stared through the darkness, a single pair of eyes shone yellow between the trees and vanished again: the herd had moved on. I must have seen half the total red deer population of that forest. Their sheer invulnerable size and the fact that they are no longer hunted of course accounts for their tolerance of humans.

All through the winter I visited Kings Ash, watching several small fallow doe herds for short periods: not till May could I come at dawn to spend a whole day with the deer.

Thin grey mist covered the land, holding every twig still. A blackbird whistled from a tall redwood and a thrush was trying out his little tunes over and over as I climbed the gate into the southern woods. They stretched away, half shrouded, up the long, mysterious slope, younger trees on this side of the road with more undercover of bramble and holly. Nothing moved, but there in front of me in a patch of bare mud was a neat, cloven hoofprint, and I knew, with a shiver of excitement, that its owner was not far away. The track was soon lost under leaf litter, but I moved on slowly, pausing by every trunk to listen and look about. No sound, not a flick of tail, till the western boundary came in sight. Beyond lay a long narrow field, cleared long ago as grazing for King's Lodge, a huge old house now lying in ruins on the far side among thickets of rhododendrons. Here, with the mist melting away in the lightening air, grazed a fallow herd, oblivious of me in the cover of the trees.

It was an interesting mix. There were three barrel-bodied does who would drop their fawns next month, they were common coated – that is, in dark brown winter coats; a still slim doe, probably an unmated yearling, and two of last year's female fawns, only slightly smaller than their mothers. According to the books, the male fawns should by now have left the herd and gone off on their own, but here was one, distinguishable by the small tassel on his belly and the two bumps on his forehead which would rapidly grow into his first pair of antlers, a simple V shape. Further down the field grazed a menil doe, her big fawn close by. Menils have lighter coats than the common. These two were a light golden brown beautifully dappled with white spots; they looked as though they had taken off their winter coats while the rest still huddled in their grey-brown winter ones.

Then there was Hoofer, who had lived in this field all winter, off and on. Something had happened to her left foreleg, so that, below the knee joint, she must carry it parallel with the ground. The black hoof end had grown out into a kind of shoe shape, some four inches long. Maybe she had been born with the hoof deformed, but it seemed more likely that she had broken the foreleg some time back, and, as it had never mended, was unable to put any weight on it. Since the toe never knew any wear and tear, perhaps it had simply gone on growing, like the claws of a dog that gets insufficient road work. In effect, Hoofer was three-legged, but she managed surprisingly well and did not look ill nourished. I had been watching her for a year and she had not been a fawn when I first saw her, so she must have survived at least three winters, though she did not appear to have mated.

The eleventh member of the herd was another who had not read the rule book about bucks going off in winter to form their own herds. This buck was slim, about three years old at a guess.

In the early morning quiet the herd was at its most relaxed. Occasionally one would lift a head, stare at the surrounding woods, then resume feeding. Well spread out over the meadow, they were grazing mostly on the far side, so that when the gate clicked and a boy came in leading two bay ponies on rope halters, they simply faded away into the rhododendron thickets which were just coming into pale, purple-pink flower (Hoofer in no way lagging behind them). The boy freed the ponies, which ambled off into a corner and began to graze. I had not lost my herd, and managed to keep one of them in sight through the binoculars all the time. Though they appear so nervous, fallow are also childishly inquisitive, and, once under cover, Hoofer had turned round to peer giraffe-necked over the shiny leaves and see what was going on, with a comical expression of affront – who dares disturb my breakfast?

Soon after the gate had clicked shut, the whole herd drifted back, lowering their heads to graze just as the sun shone out, pale and brilliant with a hint of warmth, painting the world in spring colours, lighting every detail of the deer. Except for the menils, they all looked very shabby. Most had lost some winter coat on the nape of the neck so that the bright summer auburn had begun to show through. The younger ones had patches of old coat half loosened on their haunches and shoulders. The little buck's coronets or horn bumps were already a gingery shade.

They took no notice of the ponies, one doe grazing between the two of them. After all, ponies roam the forest all the time, but it was interesting to recall this, later in the day.

Fallow wandered this land a hundred thousand years ago with straight-tusked elephant, bison and hippo, wolves and bears. (Does the race-memory of such fearsome predators lurk in every cracking twig?) Did all the deer perish in the last of the Ice Ages, only to reappear as Roman or Norman imports? No one can say for certain. I like to think that some survived in these sheltering woods to be the ancestors of *dama dama*, the fallow now living in Kings Ash.

The menil fawn suddenly stopped grazing, stared tall-necked towards the rhododendrons, grass hanging from her jaws. I have often noticed that it is the young ones in the herd who seem the most alert to danger, which is odd when they have little experience of it. Do they have keener senses than the adults? Soon eleven heads were turned westward, ears high in the five-to-one position of hands on a clock face. One of the pregnant does gave a single alarm bark, deep, short and explosive, almost like a gun shot. The whole herd turned then and raced towards the boundary where I was watching, Hoofer keeping well up with her lolloping gait, only the buck breaking away and galloping off uphill head held high. Before reaching the wire strand fence into the wood, the rest stopped, turned, bunched together and peered at the intruder who was just coming out of the opposite bushes, a woman with a small white terrier.

Twang, twang – nine twangs in all as they ducked under the lowest wire fifty yards above me where there was a deep scrape under the fence. Of course they could leap a fence twice that height with no trouble at all, but always choose to go under unless in real danger. During the first year of a fawn's life he must learn where all the scrapes are on his land; I have never seen a fallow who did not know where the quickest exits were – much used ones are betrayed by trodden paths leading to them from both sides. This scrape was a U shape a foot deep in the bank below the fence. I passed it, moving up after the deer. We were all, nearly all, in the wood together now. The buck had gone off on the other side at the top of the field, while Hoofer stayed inside, grazing still, just by the scrape, though she lifted her head from time to time, still chewing, to watch woman and dog cross the bottom of the meadow.

If only one could squint, one eye watching ahead for deer and the other scanning the ground for hazards. I moved up a narrow, leaf-strewn path, flitting from oak to chestnut, from ash to beech, peering slowly round the boles before going on. Even so, a stupid woodpigeon flew up from the beech with maximum fuss and clatter of wings. At the scrape there was not a deer in sight and the leaf litter had absorbed their hoofprints. No sound but a squabbling of crows over in the field. As I stood there listening, a female chaffinch flew down to the scrape, picked about and flew off with a thick moustache of hairs to a scrubby bank of hawthorn. Soon there were two hens, then three. They were collecting hairs from the fallow's old winter coats, brushed off in tangled hanks by the fence wire. This explained why the deer showed most new coat down the napes of neck and top of back. Chaffinches often build their nests close to each other: I once counted a terrace of five in a twenty-foot stretch of hawthorn hedge and they always line their mossy cups with hair.

Had the herd gone up the slope or spread out eastward? I could see a long way down and across the slope, where sunlight dappled the first snouts of bracken pushing up through the brown forest carpet of old leaves. The trunk of a solitary birch shone silver-white, but no dark tails flicked across white rumps, so I went on uphill, following a yellow brimstone butterfly, a bright male, which seemed a good omen. So early in the season, he must be one that had successfully hibernated through the winter.

From the crest of the hill I could see far down the south side to where the wood thinned away to a scatter of trees above a wide grassy slope, or lawn; the fallow might have been a dream. No use hurrying on, they could well be behind. So I sat down on a fallen branch to listen, and also to look out for the Stockbroker, an extraordinarily prosperous looking grey squirrel who lived in a solitary redwood nearby, its corded trunk a rich maroon-brown. It seemed an odd site to choose for a drey, since the branches all hung down and would seem to give little support, but he had kept this nest all winter and there it still stood, lodged securely some twenty feet up under the first boughs. Nothing stirred. Presently I made a hard kiss-kiss noise several times (suck the top lip down). A magpie flew past, sounding its harsh, rattling cry. Somewhere far down the slope behind, a woodpecker was drumming. Kiss-kiss.

At last the bronzy leaves of an oak whisked about, but on one branch only, and a squirrel ran along it almost to the trunk, before freezing with front paws clasped together in the 'Oh, dear me' position. It was certainly the Stockbroker, a giant as squirrels go, plump and prosperous, a wide band of gold hair beginning above his nose, sweeping down the spine and widening out up the tail, which was paler along the sides, as if frosted. When the sun lighted on him, his whole coat had a bluish tinge like an arctic fox and looked splendidly thick. When I kissed at him, he kissed back with fury; it was his temper noise. Did he know of some special diet or is this splendid physique in his genes? Did he breed super-kits? I must visit him again, but now, where are the deer? When I stood he shot straight up the oak trunk, cursing loudly. Just as well George had to be left behind this time!

Since fallow love the sun there was just a chance they might have gone to a south-facing, sheltered hollow further east, so I moved slowly along the ridge, crept downhill, lay prone and wormed my way, commando-like, to peer through scrub holly stems. There they were below in a mossy amphitheatre full of dappling sunlight filtering through sycamores in half leaf, lying down chewing the cud, even sleeping. No breeze blew my scent to them; it was a perfect viewing place, I thought. They made a real picture, only their pale lined ears moving to flick away flies, sun glinting on wet muzzles and big dark eyes. Two of the pregnant does were stretched right out with their chins on the moss, eyes closed, something you seldom see.

For some it was grooming time. The menil doe was delicately scraping the inside of one ear with her left hind hoof; a fawn turned its head to chew at a haunch, probably to dislodge a tick; one of the yearlings was concentratedly grooming its front legs, while the third doe was busy cleaning up under her tail. A pair of magpies dropped soundlessly from the canopy to land in the hollow. They strutted to and fro, staring at the deer till one flew up onto a yearling's back. Magpies often do this to probe for insects, but before it could lower its beak, the inexperienced youngster had irritably shaken it off, so it flew right away. The other magpie perched on the back of a pregnant doe and began to pull out, not succulent ticks, but a tuft of coat. The doe never twitched: the bird worked away and eventually flew off with a beakful of old brown hairs with which to line her dome-shaped nest, the light gleaming green and blue on her long, glossy tail.

A bee droned past: high above a woodpigeon 'croo-crooed' peacefully and the herd drowsed in the warm, bright air, while I lay close by. There was growing in the small of my back a cold certainty that I too was being watched: alone in the wild you learn to trust gut instincts like that. Trying not to rustle holly or dead leaves, I rolled carefully onto my side and looked round. Above me on the slope lay a long-fallen beech, and, on the top of the trunk, posed as if for his photograph, real cock-of-the-walk, stood the buck fawn, staring at me. Then he sprang into the air and gave his best attempt at an adult alarm bark; it came out a little higher in pitch, but had the same effect. The whole herd was on its feet, pronking away in stiff-legged jumps, then streaming off southward down the slope, the young buck among them, almost before I could stand up.

He had looked so engaging, perched up there! Several times I have noticed how young fallow love to be king-of-the-castle. Now the sunny wood lay empty and it was my fault for being so complacent and not counting the resting herd. I ate some sandwiches, listening the while, but felt they had gone further away this time. Past twelve, and the books say that fallow spend their afternoons lying up in deep cover; really there are no rules – I have just as often found them grazing, and the slope below offered good grass.

Even without deer it was an enchanting place, a green bank sloping down to a stream and rising steeply on the far side patched with bushes of hawthorn in brilliant white flower, matching puffs of white cloud in the blue sky above and a-twitter with little birds, a dunnock singing. Spearwort and forget-me-not reflected blurred yellow and blue in the moving stream, the frailest stems unmoving in the warm, fragrant air and, high on the far side, a flick of tail!

This was not my herd, but a lone buck, head held high but slightly sideways, a big buck in his prime, probably five or six years old, hurrying for cover because he had just lost an antler, blood still oozing from its socket – very late in the spring for this. Every adult fallow buck sheds his antlers in spring, beginning almost at once to grow a new set ready for the autumn rut. It is tempting to imagine a buck embarrassed at such a time, like a human caught with only one shoe, anxious to hide, but it is more likely to be a feeling of imbalance which makes it run for the comparative security of cover. There was just time to register a very moth-eaten looking coat before he was out of sight.

In all my forest wanderings, I have never seen a fallen antler, nor a buck chewing one, as they are said to do, for the calcium content. Of course an antler would be very hard to spot in undergrowth, but a dog might find one. George once emerged from a stand of bracken wagging the entire length of his person with joyful pride. His prize proved to be a black sheath of horn from a deer's hoof. How would he feel finding a whole antler!

Suddenly a drumming of hooves on the opposite hillside and a beautiful chestnut pony, with blonde mane and streaming tail, came into sight pursued by several fallow deer. At first I imagined this was a game, having often watched foals and young fallow playing together. But no, this seemed serious. When the pony slowed to a trot, three does chased after it, in a really belligerent manner, heads down. More deer came running up behind, agog to join in the chase. Right across the slope they belted, in and out of the blossoming hawthorns, hoof beats dying away westward till all had disappeared round a shoulder of the hill.

Whatever had the pony done to trigger such behaviour? Does are such peaceable animals with no instinct to defend territory, wandering at will into one herd and then off to another. I had never seen them act in that way even when they had very young fawns nearby and might be expected to be on the defensive. Did the pony smell peculiar in some way? I should never know. The forest is full of mysteries and here was yet one more.

Meanwhile, the fallow were slowly drifting back, spreading out over the grass, lowering heads to take a mouthful here and there, four pregnant does, several young ones, a menil and her fawn, their light coats shining gold in the sun; it was my herd, with an additional doe and her fawn, but, as afternoon shadows began to lengthen, they did not settle to feed, mooched around, stood about; two fawns sat down back to back. The young buck threw himself down and tried to rub his back in the grass, probably to dislodge the itchy old fur, but the slope of ground made him roll right over, so he scrambled up again, shaking himself and clots of old coat went flying.

Then all the herd turned their heads and stared up the slope toward the wood, though not in alarm. After a moment they began to move slowly, purposefully uphill, eleven white rumps and switching tails all turned in my direction. Had they received a silent signal, like Mole in *The Wind in the Willows*, urgently summoned back to his old home? I let them climb almost to the tree line, then followed, prudently slipping from bush to bush, but they never looked back.

From its high edge I could look far down into the sunny spaces of the wood: a small breeze had sprung up, patterning the forest floor with moving shadows, rustling the new green of beech and sycamore. High in the canopy a collared dove sang 'croo-croo-croo-CROO-croo,' over and over, two bluetits picked about in a patch of moss, and a quaking of oak leaves must be an invisible squirrel chase. I waited, on and on. At last, halfway down the long slope, a fallow walked slowly out from behind a tree, moving westward – she had been there all the time.

Before moving off to find her, something made me look down. Here at the wood's edge where sunlight could enter, more ground cover flourished, patches of gorse, and hazels with leaves still wrinkled from their unfolding. I had used a hazel for cover. Between my right foot and its small trunk sat a large bird, utterly still, lovely rufous feathers brindled with brown, paler head drawn down almost level with back, a long, long beak and dark eyes staring ahead: a woodcock, and, judging from the firm way she was bedded down, brooding eggs. How brave to hunch there all that time beside my big boot! Though I edged away as gently as possible, she stood up, stiffly as if she had sat for a long time but enough for me to glimpse roundish eggs scribbled with red brown in a mere hollow of dead leaves. Only then did she turn her head and look directly at me with hauntingly large dark eyes. I crept away, sure even from that brief glance that there were several more eggs than the four described in books.

Going down through the wood's lengthening shadows there were deer everywhere, peacefully feeding. I took root behind a beech, anxious to find out what was their favourite food at this time of year. For all the young leaves overhead, the forest floor was still predominantly brown. Two of the does were eating moss off a fallen branch, another nosed about among the small, shamrock-like leaves of woodsorrel which seldom reached flowering stage here, a fawn found some wispy grass, several were nipping off the points of bluebell leaves and the menil doe had found a patch of violets whose flowers would never now scent the air. They all avoided the largest leaves, clumps of grey-green foxglove. How did the young ones know of its bitter taste? Had they already sampled it this season, or could they tell by the smell? Nearly all the delicious new young tree leaves stood too high for them to eat, for generations of fallow had chewed off all within reach and the browse line began at about my height from the ground.

None of the available herbage suited the young buck: he attacked a young sycamore with his lower front teeth, gouging under the bark till he had loosened a flap, watched inquisitively by another yearling. Seizing the flap between bottom teeth and hard upper palate, he gave a tug, dislodging such a long strip of bark that it fell to the ground. The yearlings bent and began to eat it from opposite ends, till their wet black noses actually met, then they jumped apart and eyed each other askance! With so much other food becoming available, it might seem odd to make the effort of bark stripping, but deer often do it in the spring (to the foresters' fury) because sweet sap is rising.

Slowly the herd moved westward, I with them, creeping from tree to tree, the small breeze fortunately in my face. Once a doe looked up and straight at me, catching me on the move. I slid behind an oak and after a moment she went on grazing. I moved with them all evening through the sun-and-shadow-striped wood, an enchanted time. The young buck came quite close, so that I could see the white spotted auburn coat showing down his spine since his afternoon roll and the little fair mossy roundels on his forehead. Once he turned from grazing to look straight at me, ears flicking, and high above in the oak a cuckoo began to call in the sun's last rays.

As we neared the boundary fence to the meadow, it was my turn to disappear. I reached the gate just as ten twangs sounded through the twilight; Hoofer had company again.

When I returned later in the year to watch Stockbroker, the squirrel, and his kin, Hoofer was still grazing apparently content in the same meadow; by restricting her range she seemed to have come to terms with her three-legged state.

As I reached the crest of the wood, October mist was shredding away and soon the oaks and beeches were bathed in hazy, mellow sunshine. A dead leaf fell now and then through the still air, but the trees were not yet in their full autumn glory, only faded, with a mere shading of russet or yellow here and there. No sign of a squirrel, let alone the prosperous one, so I moved on down the slope and sat down to wait. (Needless to say, George had to stay at home again.) The previous year had been a poor one for beechmast and acorns, so squirrels had found it a difficult winter and were smaller in number. This autumn promised a bumper crop of every kind of fruit and nut in the forest, so next year there should be tails whisking round every tree.

I was sitting under a sweet chestnut, its leaves throwing long finger-shadows on the forest floor, where a few spiky green balls lay. A robin sang out from the nearest beech and a flock of chaffinches scuttered about in last year's dead leaves. A chestnut fell, splat, near my feet, then another. A nuthatch tap-tapped high in an oak and a blackbird landed nearby, scrabbling about with more noise than a badger till he caught sight of me and skimmed off with a startled 'pink-pink'. A third chestnut landed, just missing my head – and the penny dropped too. I had been slow! The nuts were not ripe enough to fall yet: they were being thrown.

Even that was not quite accurate. High in the tree a squirrel was in the act of pulling off a chestnut burr: holding the large, prickly thing carefully in its mouth, head held high, he ran back along the branch, almost to the trunk, then dropped it. In the same moment he caught sight of me, sat up straight and chittered with rage. As I did not move, he skittered off after a while, and more chestnuts came raining down beside me. Tempting to think the human interloper was actually being bombarded, but squirrels often throw nuts down in this way. It looks an efficient method: to do all the work up in the canopy, then come down to bury the harvest, rather than going to and fro with each nut. In reality, it does not work like that. The squirrel often forgets where to come down for a start, then the nuts are left for voles and woodmice. Gingerly I prized open one of the needle-sharp burrs and found a tiny, still green fruit inside. So this squirrel was being doubly wasteful, picking them before they were mature. Last year I watched a squirrel completely strip a hazel of its frilly green nut cases, when it was too early for a single one to have grown a kernel.

Wanting him to feel free to harvest his pickings, I walked on further down the slope looking for a drey and at last found one, twenty feet up, a football of twigs securely wedged between branch and bole of a beech. Sitting here in the spring on a calm morning under motionless boughs, I had been surprised to see a small branch of fresh, green leaves travelling at some speed across the floor of the forest. Presently it halted at the foot of an oak, then proceeded surrealistically straight up the trunk. The squirrel towing it was completely invisible. Did she want to strengthen her drey, was she actually ornamenting it as some birds do, or even camouflaging her home? Taking into account the harum-scarum nature of squirrels, she was probably just filling a draughty crack.

Close to the drey, I heard the unmistakable scritch-scratch of claws on bark, and hid away. Down here, near the wood's edge, a few self-seeded Scots pines had intruded. Round the trunk of one shot a skein of grey fur, winding round and up, round and up the rough bole: four young squirrels chased each other, spitting and clawing, then went out on a far branch in a flurry of waving tails and shaking branches as they threw themselves into the next tree and the next.

Presently a single squirrel appeared below the drey tree, possibly their mother. They had looked thin and scrawny, but she was plump, though without the Stockbroker's blue tinge. Flanks and head glowed copper coloured when the sun caught her fur, so it was easy to see how stories began of red squirrels returning to this forest. Of course, till the 1930s it was full of red squirrels. The old theory was that interloping greys, introduced from North America, had set upon their red cousins and exterminated them, or at least forcibly driven them away. The latest studies reckon that an epidemic caused a steep decline in the number of reds which just happened to coincide with the grey invasion. Also the red rely much more upon hazelnuts, being unable to digest acorns, so if the greys strip the hazels early in autumn, as they often do, the reds must move on. But it does seem strange that they have continued to flourish on islands such as Brownsea where the grey never landed. Perhaps they are isolated from disease also. There is a delightful story that a grey squirrel from the New Forest once boarded the ferry for the Isle of Wight at Lymington and landed on Yarmouth quay. The island people are proud of their population of red squirrels and determined to keep them, so the Harbour Master caught the offending grey, smacked its bottom and put it back on the next boat to the mainland!

My grey ran up the drey tree, right along the first branch to the thinnest twigs, swung round, returned, settled her back against the trunk to begin a thorough grooming, picking up one hind leg, then the other in her front paws to lick them over: halfway through washing her stomach fur, she remembered something urgent on the ground and had just reached the forest floor when a dog barked in the distance. She sat bolt upright, paws clasped together, frozen, for a full minute, then shot straight up the beech, hind claws in unison and disappeared far overhead through the canopy, though the dog had stopped barking some time ago.

Squirrels do not have many enemies here, apart from the forester: though they run from humans, they often go only a little way, then, like the fallow, will stop to look back and see what you are doing. They seldom seem to expect danger to fall from the air, yet their only natural predators are birds of prey, especially buzzards which nest in Kings Ash. Last spring I watched a squirrel really tempting fate, swinging through the slenderest, topmost twigs of a beech, totally exposed to the sky for half an hour, intent on biting off the sweet new tips of leaves just beginning to unfurl from their buds.

When branches above the drey began to shake, I expected the return of the four youngsters, but no, it was an adult chase, through the sweet chestnut over my head, dying away in the distance, then quickly circling back again. A small grey body leapt twenty feet into the drey tree, closely followed by another. The female, in front, squatted briefly on a wide bough, then raced off. When the male reached the spot, he paused to sniff where she had scent marked. Both flew off again, falling leaves showing their progress. Next time the female squatted, the male stopped and licked the spot. This happened several times. At last she ran out to the end of the lowest branch and the male caught up, mounting her briefly with ecstatically shaking tail.

Many books will tell you that grey squirrels mate twice a year, in midwinter and midsummer: actually they can be seen chasing and mating like this in any month of the year, but this does not mean that the female conceives every time. After this mating, they ran nonchalantly off in different directions, the male taking a huge leap from beech to oak. Occasionally they do fall from losing grip on a wet or icy branch, but usually escape unharmed.

After the Great Storm of 1987 I fought my way out to these stricken woods to try and assess what effect it had had on the forest creatures. Forestry workers did find some squirrel casualties in smashed dreys, but I came upon the most lively scene imaginable. Lower down the south slope of Kings Ash, a huge old oak had fallen; its branches meshed with lesser trees it had crashed upon and half a dozen squirrels were inspecting the damage, apparently wildly excited, skittering along the prone trunk, jumping off-on, off-on for the fun of it, chasing each other and chattering through the tangle of branches, occasionally pausing to snatch up an acorn, sit bolt upright, nibble half, then toss it away and be off again, mapping this strange, intoxicating geography of ground-level branches.

Walking back through the woods, I came upon a squirrel burying acorns. Not many had fallen yet, so perhaps she had picked these and dropped them herself. I sat down half behind a holly: the evening air was grey, full of the cheerful whistle of a late blackbird. Every now and then he called, 'Here we go, here we go!' Slowly the forest was growing dim and mysterious and vast as it always does at twilight. The squirrel dug fast with both paws, nicked an acorn with her teeth, dropped it in the hole, patted back the leaf mould, working all the time at top speed as if against a forecast of imminent blizzards. How domestic! What a splendid little house-keeper. She buried five nuts while I watched, then the efficient Mrs Beaton image was rather spoiled by her returning to the first acorn, digging it up and eating it.

When I returned here with George, he skated blithely across the frozen puddles of midwinter, while my boots cracked them apart with a noise like breaking glass. Unlikely that any squirrels would be about in the raw, cold air, but George shot off hopefully. We were on a long walk through the woods to the far western edge of Kings Ash where a south-facing slope of oaks just might harbour a herd of fallow buck. After the fever of the rutting season, bucks wander off and seem to disappear from the forest: in secluded places they form quite large groups and spend the winter together.

Bare grey trunks, brown forest floors, and in the middle a comic sight, a dachshund climbing a tree. George had managed to get three feet up the rough, slanted bole of an old leaning oak while a squirrel watched scornfully from twelve feet above. George scrabbled up another few inches. The squirrel leaned forward for a better view. George fell off. He shook his black-and-tan fur with studied nonchalance and sauntered off; hadn't really wanted the damn thing anyway.

Further on where moss made a single patch of colour round a tree stump, a fallow doe grazed with her fawn, three-quarters grown now; their dull grey-brown winter coats and pale underparts toned with the sombre woods. Bending down to graze the moss, the fawn revealed one-inch bumps or 'pedicles' on his forehead which would grow into his first antlers. Heads shot up as we passed by, but neither moved away.

Soon we came to a very odd part of Kings Ash, a wood of thin, spindly oaks, twenty feet or more high but only one foot apart. Rattling together in the slightest breeze, shining and bare, they resembled rows of clothes poles and seemed shunned at all seasons by the birds: a spooky, unnatural plantation. A forester had recently told me its history. It had been decided to use these few acres, sheltered by mature woods, as a nursery, so they were planted up with acorns, one per foot, most of which germinated, but the saplings were invaded by a plague of cockroaches. The young trees should have been transplanted to other parts of the forest, but when even the roots became infested and the whole plantation smelled of cockroach, it was abandoned.

Passing by Cockroach Grove, we came towards possible buck country, so I leashed George and tried to pad soundlessly through the dry, frost-rimmed leaves. Trees thinned towards the south, huge old pollarded oaks stood in wide glades, often with a dead, fallen limb beside them. Nothing moved. Dark twigs etched a grey sky. Too cold to sit and wait. Though in winter bucks seem to favour the ancient woodlands where there is some protection, there was little to eat. We turned north to circle back to the road, passing crow pines. Books say that a crowd of black birds will be rooks: a solitary one a crow, but for several years now, a pair of crows has lived in and around this group of six pines and, sure enough, here they were side by side, turning over the pine needles, black as night from beak to tail, black-eyed, black-legged even, hopping, feet together or stalking with dignity over the forest floor – till George chased them, that is. Is this a couple? I must come back in the spring and see if they nested together. Crows have such an evil reputation for eating eggs and nestlings of small birds, it would be good for their image to find they mated for life.

29

Leaving them to each other's company, we walked down toward a gravel track through the winter quiet, not even a robin sang or a squirrel scampered, but as we came out onto the path a commotion broke out to our right, and a group of fallow does, five of them, came tearing right past us, legs at full stretch, hooves scarcely seeming to touch the ground, eyes wide and dark with fear, closely followed by a galloping black labrador, pink tongue lolling and wildly excited. Some way behind, an elderly couple were helplessly calling, 'Benjy, Benjy!'

George stared after them, shocked. I hate to see deer chased like this. It was actually unlikely that the rather fat Labrador would ever catch a deer – they could gallop on for miles like that – and even if he did, wouldn't know what to do with it. Even so, it was a great disruption to their gentle lives. Later in the season it could even cause them to drop premature or dead fawns. If the dog were not checked now, he could do real harm come the summer when there were tiny fawns about.

'Benjy, Benjy! He's never gone off like that before,' the woman said to me worriedly, having come level. 'We only meant to let him out of the car for five minutes.'

Poor dog, no wonder he wanted a real chase. George and I hadn't a chance of catching them up, but we agreed to go back that way just to comfort the poor woman. So we set off southward toward the river, rather than northward and home, George walking at heel looking particularly smug, both of us moving fast, even jogging, to keep warm. I refused to yell 'Benjy' and create any more disturbance, besides he would probably come slinking back any minute, not being used to much exercise. The track stretched ahead monotonous and straight, but it was worth following it to the wood's edge and looking out over the heathland by the river.

We came to the gate. A vast dark landscape stretched away, dead brown heather dipping to the river hidden behind bare alder and willow, then rising beyond to a grey sky, the heath patched here and there with pale dead tussock grass or the yellow brown of bog myrtle. Dog and does might never have been. A lone gull swooped over the river, nothing else moved. But halfway down the slope, couched in deep heather, lay the buck fallow herd with their backs to us, betrayed by a forest of antlers.

Guessing that this was their winter quarters, with the river bank providing the best grazing for miles, I came back next day without George. Yes, there they were (and blessings on you, Benjy, whatever your sins). Cold though it was, these were perfect deer-watching conditions, for I could stay just inside the wood with the south-west wind in my face and look right down on the herd. Under a washy blue sky, they were widely scattered across the slope, grazing with their heads down so that it was not possible to see their antlers well, but there seemed to be two really big bucks, eight or nine of slighter build and half a dozen younger ones. In theory it is supposed to be possible to tell a buck's age from its antlers, since every year its new set should have an extra point on each side, but in practice it is much more difficult. Once an animal has passed its prime, its antlers tend to get smaller with the years. Also it can be tricky to decide which are the largest antlers in a herd – the tallest or the most widely palmated?

By noon the sun had struggled weakly out. One by one the bucks stopped grazing, wandered around in an apparently haphazard way, then somehow found themselves close together and sank down among the old heather bushes in a tight group, facing the river to chew the cud, rather like club members relaxing in their armchairs after a heavy meal. At last it was possible to see the antlers rather well.

There was just one pricket, with the simple V shape of a fallow in its second year, the only one possible to date with accuracy. After him came a whole group with well branched, but narrow antlers; I guessed them to be three-year-olds, each beam or side antler having a brow tine (that is, a spike) facing forwards, another above it, then a straightish branch ending in a rough V shape at the top. In the senior group, antlers grew out sideways before turning upwards and widening out into a flattened palm with many points or 'spellers', handsome heads that would have been quite impressive seen on their own, but dwarfed by the magnificent spread of the two older or king bucks, holding their heads so proudly even while ruminating, though this is probably all a matter of balance. Out across the dun-coloured heath, a figure appeared with a dot of white dog (I never did see Benjy again) and they all watched or smelled its progress; I could tell by their parallel muzzles, though the jaws went on moving in a leisurely way. Walker and dog moved off; a magpie sounded its harsh rattle from the woods; thin cloud broke here and there to reveal patches of cold blue sky: the deer seemed settled for their afternoon rest.

Hearing an odd noise behind me, I found myself under the annoyed scrutiny of a squirrel, ten feet away; perhaps I was standing on his acorn cache. He was sitting in a young beech with his haunches on one branch and his front paws on one a little higher, showing off an expanse of snow-white chest and tum, switching his tail constantly to and fro like an angry cat and making a sound rather like a duck; squirrels really do have the most surprising range of vocals. I refrained from answering back or moving, so he continued to quack till the sound rose to a chattering scream and he flew up the tree, right over my head and swung off into the wood.

On the river slope, two of the senior bucks have stood up. Without seeming to notice each other, they potter away from the herd a few yards, stand gazing into space for a bit, then whirl round and stare at each other. Each then advances slowly, stiff-legged till within striking range, lowers his head and charges. Antlers clash and crash together, taut back legs straining forward for maximum shoving power. They seem exactly matched, for neither gives an inch. At last they disengage, have a short staring match, then charge again. A few of the herd look round, mildly interested at the loud noise of bone on bone. This time their antlers become locked together, so they have to shake their head to disengage. Once parted, they pause only a moment before beginning again. Now the nearer buck gives ground, is pushed back a full yard, but seems in no way beaten in spirit, pronking off with arched back, then kicking out his back legs, dancing almost, for this was what I had hoped all along to watch, a winter play-fight, a game, entirely without the murderous passions of the autumn rutting combats.

Several more of the senior bucks were getting to their feet, eyeing a possible playmate. One pair advanced toward each other as in slow motion, chins almost touching the ground. Soon the air was loud with the sound of clashing antlers from four or five amiable duels going on at once. The pricket took no part, though the three-year-olds were at it. One of the king bucks rose ponderously to his feet, watched the nearest fight for a time, then sank down again.

Some of the fights were draws; in others, one would eventually give ground before returning to the fray and making his opponent retreat. The pair who had begun broke off first, wandered back to the herd side by side and sat down. The stiff-legged pronk or bounce is often an alarm reaction, but in this context it seemed to be a mere antic, indulged in by victor and vanquished alike. It was delightful to watch and presumably has some training value for the younger bucks.

Cloud covered the sky again, the sun a faint dull, orange blur in the west. A chill mist began to gather along the river valley as far trees became black silhouettes and early winter dusk crept over the heath. As the deer began, two by two, to retire to the herd, a vision of a log fire, hot tea and toast arose before me, but, just as I was about to turn for home, to my surprise, the two king bucks stood up, moved away side by side, faced up to each other and charged, with a heart-stopping thwack of those huge antlers. Several wood-pigeons flew up from their roosts alarmed by the shock of it. Three times the giants clashed together, each hurling himself forward, neither giving way a twig's width, then, honour satisfied, they stalked majestically back through the twilight to the herd, antlers high.

Play was over for the day.

BUCKLAND WATER

A WILD green and blue world of howling wind, racing cloud shadows and plunging white wings: an April gale at the mouth of Buckland Water. Waves broke in great fountains of spray on the shingle bank precariously knitted together by sea spinach, grey purslane and spring beauty just opening its fragile flowers in this wilderness of winds and stones. Overhead a tern struggled with the surging currents of air to reach its nest down there on the bare shingle, trying to keep beak to wind but constantly being tossed sideways. The gale swept past me, full of clamorous bird cries and salty foam.

News had come that a pair of roe deer, most elusive of all the deer breeds, were living in Whiteoak Woods along the higher reaches of the river, so I felt driven to walk its whole length, from mouth to source. Who could tell what wonders Buckland Water might spring? To me it was as exciting as the Amazon.

Blackheaded gulls were trying to fly in, but so tossed about the blue sky, they were forced to flutter their wings like tern. Those that made it had energetic bathing sessions in huge puddles on the rutted track: they will always seek out fresh water. If one trespasses on another's bath territory, each sinks dark head below wing level and menaces the other with wide open maroon beak and raucous screams. A flock of little dunlin skittered about the tide edge, jerky as clockwork toys, and an oyster catcher flashed past peeping urgently as if late, a reminder to move on, upriver.

This was not possible for a moment, as something intimate was taking place on the track. A pair of ringed plover were trying to mate: beautiful little birds with white collars, black bibs and orange legs. The male mounted several times but was blown off again. At last he managed to stay put, but had constantly to extend a wing, first on one side, then on the other, to keep his balance. Finally the female sensibly trotted off the track and down the landward bank, out of the wind's way, carrying her mate on her back!

The river mouth was a sparkling, exhilarating place, but it was a relief to turn inland, out of the buffeting winds and look upriver to the familiar sheltering edge of woodland. Below the shingle bank and in the lea of a wide gorse brake in full bloom, stretched a vast green marshy meadow where hundreds of birds had settled to wait out the gale so that now I walked between the river and a sea of birds. A whole flock of lapwing rested on the grass, with some twenty oyster catchers, smart in their black-and-white, and a dozen curlew. Near the path a shelduck sat fast asleep, head turned back under wing, never twitching a feather as I moved past, while others were parading up and down, bobbing heads and displaying to their mates.

I thought part of the gorse had been burnt, leaving only black sticks, till several of them stood up! I have been taken in before by Brent geese; they sit so still and tall necked. A whole flock of these small, dark geese moved slowly across the meadow towards the river, murmuring to each other in deep gentle croaks, white rumps visible. Soon tall reed beds walled off the sea-world of the Point and I was able to fetch George. Till then I had been in a bird reserve, where even people must have permits, let alone dogs, though George once visited a hide there as a puppy – in the warden's pocket.

No longer tidal, the river now ran broad and clear, four feet deep, over a stony bottom, hung with huge old willows breaking into silvery leaf, and a few gnarled oaks in golden green. Lush banks sprouted hemlock water dropwort, rough comfrey leaves and square-stemmed figworts. The first red campions were out, a single yellow iris and a whole bank of primroses, flowering late in the willow shade.

Round a bend, the river widens into a pool, where a fallen oak branch hangs over the water. Ranged along its top are five infant coot, skinny little black things with bright yellow beaks, red foreheads and pale necks, much more like moorhen than their real mother who is just walking out onto the branch, bobbing her white face shield. She pauses to look along the row like a teacher gathering attention, then dives into the water, swims away a few feet, and turns to wait for the fledglings to follow suit. One scratches its left ear, otherwise they all sit immobile; they could have been stuffed. She swims round for a time then returns to the branch, dives off, flies straight back and looks along the row again. She is wonderfully patient; could easily tip them all in with her beak. She dives again, this time swimming off upstream till she is out of their sight, but the five still huddle there, eyeing the current of sun-spangled water with deep suspicion, till number three with the itchy ear stands up to scratch, loses his balance and falls with a startled 'kohk' into the river.

Instantly mother returns, circles baby who is valiantly swimming against the stream, and everyone gets the message. Plop, plop and they are all in the water. Mother paddles off into the sheltering willows, the small flotilla close behind.

Soon we passed through a six-foot gate in an equally tall fence, for the next wood, Cuckoo Copse, was a nature reserve, fenced against grazing animals, and what a difference! Bluebells stretched away across the forest floor, hazing even the distance with colour, drifting a sweet, gentle fragrance on the air. Round the mossy roots of oaks, the delicate white stars of wood anemones mingled with varnished yellow celandines and wood violets. Hawthorn and hazel, out in new leaf, were green from almost ground level, unbrowsed, with honeysuckle bines twining every trunk above the shining arrow heads of wild arum.

So, if the deer were kept out, the whole forest would be full of scent and colour . . . no, I would not change it. In spite of the pretty flowers, the wood lacked excitement without the possibility of glimpsing deer. Blackbirds sang at each other, bluetits and chaffinches twittered and fussed and a wren set up a loud, ticking alarm. I located it in a hawthorn, where its mate flew urgently to join in, two tiny, indignant birds, tails up straight with temper. They must surely have a nest close by, to be so upset. Then I became aware that George, on a lead as prescribed by reserve rules, was looking up in a puzzled, considering sort of way, quite without the manic glee reserved for squirrels.

Almost above our heads, strung along a low bough, perched six baby wrens, even smaller than their parents, but fluffy feathered, each sitting frozen-still while mum and dad grew more and more frantic. They regarded me with sharp little eyes, motionless, till in the end one tried an alarm call. It came out softer and higher pitched than the parents' staccato. We left them to calm down.

Another tall gate brought us into the forest proper; not a tree here with leaves below five feet, the floor a sea of dead leaves, barren and bare, relieved only by the green of moss. This was deer country. In fact, following the river had brought us to the edge of Kings Ash, so it was worth making a small detour to check if the red herd had returned to their usual resting place. We were approaching from the west this time, so had to crawl through the rhododendron bushes and over the black earth between them. Almost through, I stood up cautiously and gazed out across the leathery leaves. No ponies moved today out on the swampy heath; bushes of bog myrtle in scaly bud burned orange in the sun and a single lark sang, high overhead.

The small movement almost under my nose must be a bird, a rabbit? No, it was an ear. Four feet away across the last rhododendrons a brown ear twitched. Craning forward I could see tops of heads, napes of necks. The red hind herd were chewing their cud, bedded down in tall dead heather bushes with this thicket at their backs to shelter them from the prevailing wind, drowsing in the sun, oblivious of me and even of George. Still in their brown winter coats, they were difficult to distinguish from the heather brooms. A long wait. Tied to a low branch, George went to sleep. More larks sang. Finally, anxious to make out the composition of the herd, I coughed gently. No one stirred. A louder cough had no effect either. I didn't want to alarm them, but I did want them to stand and be counted; even to see them stretch their necks and look round would help.

'Wake up!' I called. They drowsed on. 'Come on, George, bark a bit,' I suggested.

With the unerring dachshund nose for maximum comfort, he had found the one spot where sunlight filtered through the thick leaves, and slept on, snoring faintly.

Red deer are only belligerent at rutting time; even then it is only the stags that grow bad tempered, so I could go and walk among them, but this would alarm the herd too much and they would be off before I could count them. In the end I stood, jumped up and down, and waved my notebook – a funny sight for any passing lark that happened to glance down. One hind did look round, but the rest went on chewing placidly.

Then, all of a sudden, a single deep bark brought every deer to its feet. I had seen or heard nothing to alarm them, perhaps an eddy of breeze wafted them dog-scent. Before I could count, they were bounding away down the thicket line, soon lost to view, never having caught sight of me. I did manage to see, among all the hinds and their calves, one huge old stag with a grey face and the forehead bumps or pedicles of new antlers, just beginning to grow, like an elderly male admirer tolerated by the Mothers' Union. Was he the limping stag, last of the herd I had seen in November? It seemed likely. Soon they had all disappeared into the darkness of a pine wood to the north.

Time to press on upriver, for we were approaching roe country, the fringes of Whiteoak Woods. Unlike red, fallow and sika, roe are not fond of grass, though they will eat it: their favourite food is bramble shoots and briar. Here the river flows down through ancient open oak woods, the trees wide spaced because many were pollarded ages ago and, with their main stems removed, have spread huge branches out sideways, parallel with the ground. Some are so old they are dying back, 'stag-headed', as the foresters say, their topmost boughs sticking up above the new spring canopy, bare as antlers. Others have fallen in winter storms to leave wide gaps where the sun can stream through, enabling bushes to grow.

On a warm May morning, the sunny, grassy glades are drifted with hawthorn scent and lightened by the queer flowers of wood spurge, vivid pale green discs, above dark green leaves on rose madder stems, never eaten by deer, so flourishing in groves. Without George that day, I settled down on the trunk of a fallen oak, beside the river with a long view up through the woods, a faint breeze in my face, enticing bushes of bramble and briar spread about the slope and little prospect of disturbance by walkers since there was no path here.

Up the long slope, nothing moved, but close by over the river a sudden flash of brilliant blue and a kingfisher arrowed past. I longed to follow, and look for her tunnel nest in the bank, but stayed on my tree trunk, itself a little garden. Where the bole fanned out into sky-pointing roots the tiny white flowers of wood sorrel grew, with inch-high dog violets and struggling young foxglove plants all bedded in deep moss, and grey-green lichen studded with minute cups, trailed over with young ivy. Across the river, a rustle in the nearest oak and a squirrel came down the trunk, sat up to clean his whiskers in a leisurely way, then ran along the bank to a bare root, seized it in one paw and swung down onto a six-foot crescent of shingle beach where the river curved round a bend. Here

he leant forward and sipped delicately for about a minute, something I've rarely seen.

But up the long slope, nothing moved. Afternoon now: not good deer-spotting time, they are most often lying up in cover (though I should know better than to make rules), so I decided to move on up to a clearing where roe are said to come out to feed in the evening.

The bank became a swamp with widely spaced tussocks of grass separated by dark, oozing mud, so treacherous it bore not so much as a mouse print . . . Halfway across, teetering on a six-inch island, trying to get my balance before the next jump, the mud making slurping noises, I became aware that a spindly holly bush some twenty feet away had too many trunks – thirteen in fact. In its shade, three fallow does were watching my flounderings with absorbed interest.

Fallow are always a delight to come upon, but to find them here boded ill for seeing roe, or so I thought at the time, since roe, being the smallest of the deer in this forest, are said to feel threatened by any of the other species and avoid their company. When I did reach firm ground, the girls had not moved, so, as I was not going to stay and had nothing to lose, I opened a conversation with a short bark.

Silence. Blackbirds were singing overhead. Then one doe barked back, without moving away. In all we exchanged four barks each with perhaps half a minute's wait between mine and hers. It was always the same doe who replied. In the end, all four stalked off, whisking tails over white rumps, not hurrying, apparently unalarmed.

Upriver then. Gnats danced over the water, shadows lengthened through the wood. Later in the month it would be even more difficult to find roe, because the doe would be hiding away in deep cover for the birth of her twins, with the buck nearby. Unlike other deer, roe live in family groups nearly all the year round, similar to the typical British family, mum, dad and the two children. The river, narrowing now to a mere stream, emerged from the woods, curving round inviting little lawns sheltered by thorn thickets. Through a straggle of branches I caught a flick of tail again, edged nearer, peered through.

Just on the other side of the stream was a big herd of fallow, perhaps twenty does and yearlings. Some drowsed on the grass, chewing the cud, some grazed the juicy spring grass, while others browsed the tops off new hawthorn: what we used to call 'bread and cheese' as children. At last they had lost their dull winter look, and made a fine picture in their white-spotted chestnut coats. In the middle of the herd, stretching up to a thorn, was a pure white doe, reminding me of Wordworth's poem 'The White Doe of Rylstone' where poor Emily Norton of Rylstone has lost her whole family in the Rising of the North, her sole consolation being the company of a gentle white doe. After her death the faithful creature visits her grave among the ruins of Bolton Abbey every Sunday:

> Comes gliding in with lovely gleam
> Comes gliding in serene and slow,
> Soft and silent as a dream
> A solitary doe.
> White is she as lily of June,
> And beauteous as the silver moon.

All my does were beautiful though. Eating bread and cheese I watched them through the thorns, a light breeze blowing my scent away, intent not to disturb them. Some must be heavily pregnant with fawns to be dropped next month, yet they kept their figures so well it was not easy to pick out the expectant mothers, and even last year's fawns, now almost yearlings, were nearing adult size. The small males often go off alone at the end of the winter, but here were two grazing close together both with very small V-shaped antlers still in velvet which would go on growing till August, not shed in the spring like the adults, but will then be retained till the following summer. All the time antlers are growing, they are covered by a thick velvety skin which contains essential nerves and blood vessels. As soon as the antler is full grown, the velvet becomes redundant and is stripped off.

I contemplated crawling past the thicket on all fours: even so, as soon as I was upriver of them, the wind would bring my scent to those sensitive black noses. In the end I walked away from the river at a right angle for a hundred yards, then moved on parallel with it, steadily, watching sideways. As I came into view every head went up, ears alerted in the five-to-one position, though jaws went on chewing. It only needed one to panic and they would all bolt. Two does knelt up, stood, as I drew level. A yearling came several steps forward, right to the river bank, head weaving from side to side, testing the air for danger. Ten yards and they were still rigid, watching my back. But twenty yards and they were beginning to relax, heads lowering to graze again. One can often pass deer openly like this by keeping an easy pace and not overtly staring at them.

I came back to Buckland Water at a much loved spot. Here the river curved round a little circular lawn, backed by a half-moon of hawthorn; on the opposite bank, young willows overhung the water. Last summer I came here to picnic and dabble my feet after a long, hot walk — to find a paradise of colour hidden away, tall flowering rush with umbels of deep rosy pink flowers, spikes of purple loosestrife and, on the slack stream, the small yellow water lilies called brandy bottles. I had always wanted to test this name: did the flowers really smell of brandy? In such a secluded spot it should be easy to lie prone and get a sniff, but I could not after all disturb the damsel fly which added a final touch of brilliance; she was a shining emerald green, with wings to match, patrolling the yellow lilies in search of a blue male, while a black-and-white wagtail flicked about the willows.

The hawthorn was clotted with pale flowers, loud with bees and hoverflies. A curlew's haunting cry floated out over the heath. Buckland Water was only a three-foot stream, winding and slow, dark with trailing stems of water weed and the floating oval leaves of pond weed with tiny silver fish darting through them in shoals. Ahead the land rose, close forested. Somewhere up there should I find my elusive roe and the source of my Amazon?

First, though, the late sun slanted through a narrow belt of pines planted on a steep bank. Scrambling up, I came to a grassy plain called Lady Garden, pausing just inside the trees to watch rabbits come out for their evening frolic and feed. Three half-grown ones grazed together; one large rabbit was intent on grooming his ears, pulling first one then the other down for a good lick over; another seemed restless, hopping about for a quick bite here and there, while a dozen more were settled to feed, scattered about between the gorse bushes in the first shadows of evening, a placid, peaceful scene till a muffled double stamp–thud, thud–sent every single one racing for the nearest burrow in a flurry of white scuts. Dark wings passed overhead through the conifer branches. I could not identify the shape: it was most likely a buzzard for they do nest up here. Almost at once the rabbits came out again, in twos and threes, sitting in their burrow mouths for a moment, then hopping off to feed again.

Then I became aware that a particularly plump rabbit, probably a pregnant doe, was moving in a most extraordinary manner–on its back! Right in front of me this large rabbit was moving steadily along the contour of the bank, white belly upward; such an astonishing sight I could not for a moment work out what was happening. Jumping the stream, scattering rabbits in all directions, I ran after the surreal animal, realizing that it must be dead and being towed along from the other side. When I came closer the rabbit was swiftly turned through a right angle without a pause and dragged straight up the slope. As it disappeared into the gorse I glimpsed a streak of auburn fur, a stoat. It seemed incredible that so small an animal could actually tow a fat rabbit at all, let alone at that speed: what's more the kill must have taken place right under my nose without my having seen a thing.

I could have stayed there watching them, but the source must be found before dark. Little more than a ditch now, Buckland Water formed the boundary between conifers and open ground, disappeared into a culvert under a wide grass ride then reappeared on the other side in Swines Wood, one of the oldest parts of the forest. All this way and no sight of roe deer. A jay screamed at me, flew off with a flash of blue wing feather. The woodland floor was striped with long tree shadows of oak and beech; scattered yew trees already stood in pools of darkness and a tawny owl called his long bubbling 'hoo-hooo' close by, beating his bounds. I peered into the ditch for the gleam of water – was this the undramatic source of my river, a ditch running dry? But something made me look up again.

From the darkness beneath a nearby yew, I was being watched. There were two small faces side by side, pale, suspicious, each with that unmistakeable patch of black beside the nose, then, soundlessly, they vanished. The roe deer had found *me*.

It was late May before I could return to Swines. Meanwhile my spies had said, yes, there was a pair of roe there with twins. While I had walked upriver the hard way, the other side of it had a car park beside a busy road. Obviously the deer would be deep inside so I decided to take George for a run close by before setting out alone. Swines was a vast territory–the hunt could take days.

Very early on a warm, still morning we walked down into the woods, old beech and oak wide spaced and everywhere sunlit grassy glades, the trees just in new leaf, bracken waist high with tips still curled over, a green world full of bird song. George trees two squirrels while I take a long, slow sweep through the glasses down the slope – and quite close there is something tawny brown standing in the next glade. I kneel down and at once George leaves his latest victim, spitting with rage twelve feet up an oak, and comes to be leashed. I dare not risk taking him back to the car, the deer could so easily disappear in that time. So George was with me all through that extraordinary morning.

May had been a warm, dry month, but this meant that every leaf on the forest floor was crisped into a little dry roll emitting maximum crackle when stepped on. This made stalking very slow and hazardous: it really was quite impossible to be silent. We tried to creep down over the grass to the stand of trees overlooking the next clearing. In the middle of it was a clump of scrub hawthorn and holly with deer grazing on the far side. I set out to flank them, still under cover of the trees, setting down one foot at a time, slowly, till a flick of tail betrayed that they were fallow. Impossible to be disappointed when they looked so beautiful in their chestnut and white, grazing so content, beside – what was that under the hawthorn? Two does moved about the grass, but lying down by the thicket was a little thing, ears twitching, head up.

Fawns were not usually born till June and this did not look by any means new born. Fawn-like, its coat was paler than the adults, but for a long time it refused to stand up and reveal its true size. Overhead, a woodpigeon sang 'croo-croo-croo-CROO-croo' and not a leaf moved till my attention was caught by a peculiar movement somewhere over to the left, a glimpse of something swinging to and fro. Could it be a roe buck fraying? In May they are said to change territories and so need to mark out new boundaries. One way of doing this is to swing antlers violently at some small tree, stripping leaves and twigs, leaving it looking frayed. We could probably return to the fallow later for a proper look at the young one. Today it was roe that really mattered.

We set off through the trees toward the swinging and soon saw the cause, a bay pony having a delirious roll in the grass, long legs semi-circling the air! Stalking the pony had brought us to the bottom of the narrowest part of the wood where it bordered a private estate protected by an eight-foot deer fence. A series of open glades and stands of great oak and beech bordered it, north and south. Looking south through the trees I could see an empty glade, then a second one with a pony in its centre – very thin-legged, deep rust-brown . . . through binoculars I could see it was a red deer, a stag with half-grown antlers, and beside him, lying in the grass, something very small, rufous red, which must be a calf. The stag should have been miles away in a bachelor herd for the summer and whoever heard of a calf with its *father* rather than its mother? I can only describe what I saw in Swines Wood, not explain it. When I lowered the glasses, stag and calf were gone.

They could only have moved round behind a thicket near the fence. I slipped urgently from tree to tree, frantic to get a better look at this totally surprising pair. Where was mother? A wren shot out of the nearest oak 'tick-ticking' indignantly. We circled round till the clearing was in full view – and empty. Best wait then, really we had been crashing about too much already. I settled down at the base of an oak, on its mossy root-hump: since this could mean a picnic, George settled down too. We were in deep shade, but the clearing was full of sunshine, lit like a stage waiting for the performance to begin. A nuthatch 'tap-tapped' overhead and all around chaffinches were singing from the boughs.

Then the first performer enters; I hold my breath with delight. A roe deer steals out onto the grass, looks carefully round and, after a moment, lowers her head to graze. At last! My first chance simply to watch: all other sightings had been mere glimpses. She was smaller than a fallow doe, with a sandy gold coat, very tall ears set high, a buff-coloured rump patch and a mere apology of a tail, just a little tab. A rustle at the edge of the glade made me look across just in time to see the roe buck come running into the clearing. He stopped abruptly beside the doe and began to graze with her, his short antlers, with three points on each side, shining in the sun.

Only the twins were missing, probably lying up in the bracken nearby. Never mind, I could watch all day, follow when the doe went to feed them. A pity about George, but he was being very good, watching the deer with mild interest though looking pointedly at my pocket from time to time. They soon moved behind a bank of blackthorn and scrub willow, keeping close together, till the buck wandered out again and began to browse new leaves off the lowest beech bough. Soon the doe moved out onto the grass too; if she were about to feed the twins, how could I follow her without stampeding the buck? But she was only walking over to join her mate.

Of the red stag and calf there was no sign: I never saw them again, but they remain like a snapshot in the mind.

Up in the canopy a blackbird was whistling away. Just as he was cheerfully singing 'here we go!' his note changed to the 'pink-pink' of alarm and a party of holidaymakers came crashing and laughing through the wood. The roe had bounded away in an instant, vanishing to the north.

If there were kids here, the mother at least would have to return, though not at once probably, so I stood up and walked across to the side of the clearing where the doe had first appeared. In theory you find her track and follow it to the resting babies. Actually the whole wood was criss-crossed with narrow tracks winding between bracken stands and the ground dappled with leaf shadow that moved softly now and then over patches of tawny old leaves so that searching was very difficult, just as it should be, from the deer point of view. 'Find them!' I urged George and he put his nose to ground at once, pulling me along – but only towards the nearest squirrel. For a time we moved quietly about, searching, finding only small woodland flowers, cow-wheat, tormentil, late violets, till it seemed best to return to the oak-seat and wait.

A worrying thought: had my informants mistaken the group of fallow for parent roe and their offspring? If there were no kids, there was nothing to bring the roe pair back here. The doe had not looked pregnant, but I did not know how obvious it might be with roe. A weasel ran along the fence bank: two young squirrels played tag, over and back, across a fallen tree trunk, and George was sorely tried. Perhaps there was another pair with kids in the wood, but where? What nonsense then that roe never shared their chosen country with the larger fallow. The blackbird was whistling again. Shadows crept across the clearing. A far rustle made me seize the glasses, gaze hopefully north, but the sound soon became thundering hooves. Two mares came crashing through the wood closely followed by a stallion, eyes rolling, a handsome chestnut with blonde mane and tail. After all that commotion it seemed unlikely the roe would return, so we left, for that day.

Nothing equals that first moment of entering a wood in the early morning, this wild green place seething with secret life where I was the intruder. It was cool, sunny and breezy. Two teenage squirrels raced through the beech boughs overhead, chasing a third with a nut in its mouth, sending down showers of copper-coloured leaf bracts on my head. In the same glade as the previous day, at the foot of the slope, two fallow does were grazing, though a little

restless: they kept standing stock still and gazing off southward. A pale stump of wood at the foot of the hawthorn flicked an ear, so the young one was still in there and this must be the same fallow group. As the does came to lie down close by, the clearing was invaded by a whole family of jackdaws, five of them, which spread out in a line and approached the deer. One went up to the nearest doe's rump and began to probe her fur for insects; at first she took no notice but eventually he dug too deep and she swung her head round. He hopped away two feet, then came back to start again.

I turn south towards the roe glade, hoping that they too are creatures of habit and at once see a roe, too close, standing at right angles to me, quite still, in bracken. I peer through the glasses to see if she is feeding her young, but no. Presently she moves slowly away, ambling about the wood, pausing now and then to browse small thorn bushes. Each time she's finished with one, she rubs her face against the twigs before moving on. Twice she turns and glances at me, where I lie flat in the grass, but seemed unconcerned. When I am forced to sniff, in lieu of blowing my nose, she hears and twitches her tall ears. As she crosses an open patch it is plain she is not yesterday's sandy doe, but one with a darker, more foxy-coloured coat and a pale amber behind. Why is the buck not defending his family territory? Whose territory is it?

Afraid of getting too close, I line up an ancient oak bole wide enough to hide three people, between us. When I reach it and carefully peer round, she has vanished, so I sit down at the foot of an oak and wait in a chill breeze. Three baby bluetits sit in line on a branch above my head. When mother returns with a beak full of squirming things, they lean forward eagerly, vibrating their little wings, but she disappears into a fissure in the trunk and after a moment of stunned surprise they all whizz in after her. Presently I am forced to walk on, just to warm up. No deer anywhere. Think longingly of flask of hot coffee in car and turn back to cross the roe clearing, when something small, lanky and golden streaks across the top of the glade – and is gone. A fawn kid – one of the twins! Infant roe, and fallow, are programmed to lie still in deep cover till their mother returns to feed them: even a visit from a large human will not normally cause them to stir. Certainly I had not startled the kid for it is running half towards me and there is no sign of mother, so what had scared it out of hiding? It seems to have taken refuge behind the branches of a fallen tree, but does not reappear, though I watch a long time.

A thrush is singing high in the beech above my head, trying out his various tunes wonderfully clear and sweet: he seems to have a repertoire of at least seven different phrases. When at last I stand up, the darker roe female is visible some way down the fence, browsing hawthorn with her back to me, but it is time to go. As I turn away, there is a small movement, a flick of sandy-gold up by the fallen tree, so I move very slowly and quietly through the sun-spangled shadows and peer round. Very close is an anxious little face, big dark eyes gazing away from me towards mother. I tiptoe away, coming upon a group of ponies. Did one of them stumble over the kid and cause it to bolt?

Halfway up through the trees a quick movement ahead sends me diving behind an oak, just in time to see my original sandy doe running down the slope, followed by the buck, who catches her up. Following them back to 'their' glade, I lose the buck but the doe makes for a fallen tree and pauses in among the dead branches for a good groom, paying particular attention to her forelegs, then rubbing her muzzle and forehead repeatedly on the bare twig ends; it looks painful, but she appears to enjoy it. The buck does not reappear: he is the same sandy colour as the doe. Is the darker one his mate as well? Sandy doe is having a delirious scratch between the eyes and shows no sign of going off to feed any kids. Overhead the thrush is shouting 'Big ears, big ears!' When people and dogs begin to invade this narrow corner, he and the doe vanish and it is no use staying any longer.

Out in the world it is a sunny Sunday, the air warmed up now: as I near the car park there are shouts, laughter and the smack of ball on bat, and something else – a small oak shaking violently and a body blundering noisily away on the far side. Sidling round I come face to face with a roe buck, a spray of new oak leaves poking from his jaws. Five yards away on the other side of some gorse, a picnic party is noisily setting out chairs and baskets; so much for all the stories of roe deer only to be found deep in woods far from human disturbance! It is not as if young oak were in short supply. This buck has slightly shorter horns than the sandy one: presumably he belongs to the darker doe. He bounds away, then stops to look back, allowing me to see that his coat is the darker, foxy red shade.

'I did pack the tomatoes,' someone is shouting close by.

Two pairs of roe to watch, if only everyone would go home!

Roe and fallow probably felt the same, for next day there was no sign of either. The woods were threaded by ancient cart tracks, the narrow ridges beside them a little higher than the rest of the forest floor, so that dead leaves tended to blow off, leaving a bare mossy strip, just wide enough to pad along silently. In fallow glade and roe glade, nothing stirred at ground level though the wood was full of flickering wings and bird song. When a jay flashed past and disappeared into thick oak foliage, setting up a clamour of squeaky cries, I realised that he had a nest in there, though jays usually prefer scrubby trees. Chaffinches were singing all around; then, just as the blackbird whistles 'here we go,' something rustles among the fern.

It is a hare, not a creature one expects to meet in a wood. It runs slowly up the cart track towards me, turns aside to nibble some grass, moves nearer till a mere six feet away, wanders round me without seeming to notice my presence and potters off, feeding as it goes. I have never had so close a view of the dark chestnut fur and black-tipped ears. Is the animal sick, to be so relaxed at my presence? But by the end of the morning the wood is full of hares, ambling about, sampling grass here and there, wandering from sun to shade, shade to sun, all seemingly content and unafraid. They never look directly at me, but pass by or let me overtake them; it is delightful to be accepted as an honorary hare. One pauses a few feet away and decides to have a groom, drawing each long ear down in turn and giving it a thorough licking over, then doing the small of the back, which is more difficult, finally washing the face with licked front paws.

Then it rained and rained, though the downpour had reduced to drizzle when I returned to Swines. At least it was easier to move about quietly now, though the wood looked dull and gloomy. There was no sign of fallow in their glade, so I moved silently on from oak to oak, towards the roe's. It was a temptation to hurry on and try to find them somewhere else: always a mistake. Every now and then an extra heavy spatter of raindrops spilled from the canopy, sounding like the patter of feet on the woodland floor. I reached the last oak overlooking the glade, peered at the roe's favourite thicket up the long slope. Only squirrels were playing in a far dim aisle between the beeches, so I stepped out from cover meaning to skirt the clearing and go down the fence, but there is a female roe straight ahead, materialized out of nowhere, gazing at me with wary dark eyes. If she bolts, the day is ruined.

I freeze, then back slowly to the cover of some scrub hawthorn and sink on to the grass. She watches my manoeuvres with interest, at last lowers her head to graze – and I can breathe again. Will she lead me to the twins? This is the sandy one. I stalk her for half an hour as she meanders through the wet woods. The bluetit mother flies to her nest hole, welcomed by an appreciative chorus of high squeaks. When the doe heads uphill in the direction of that hideously busy main road, I let her go, afraid of possibly bolting her towards danger, and return to the space between thicket and fence which she frequents so often. Could the kids be there?

Of all the choice green spaces the forest has to offer this area is, at least from the human point of view, the pits: quite literally, for along the fence lie a series of ugly bare hollows, strewn with dead branches and a few scrappy thorn bushes, certainly no cover for young ones. Further along the formidable fence, where the wood narrows, there is a tree stump green with moss and small sprouts of bilberry, partly drifted with dead leaves, with a ring of bare earth trodden all round it – a roe dancing floor where the buck has chased the doe round and round during the rut. Back in the roe glade, a young crow, quite as big as his parents, is wagging his wings and demanding raucously to be fed. What is endearing behaviour in an infant bluetit looks plain comic in a bird that size. Sandy moves and reveals herself again, in the pits, browsing hawthorn shoots, occasionally just staring into space or at me. I am not hidden, though leaning against an oak to break my outline and in its deep shade, for the sun has come out at last: big blobs of shredding cloud send shadows flying through the woods.

Looking through the glasses to see if there is any sign of the kids, I see another sandy shape half hidden in bracken, but too large. Presumably it is the original buck, though twigs obscure antlers. Sliding sideways for a better view I discover there are no antlers: it is the darker doe, sitting with her back to me. Sandy ambles about, rubbing her forehead against the ends of dead branches, then sitting down to chew the cud beside her friend.

This seems extraordinary behaviour when roe are said to keep in close family groups of male, female and offspring, with the buck constantly marking his territory by scrapes and frays. Was this buck polygamous, or was the extra doe last year's kid who had failed to leave the family as she should have done in May? A movement off to the left causes both does to stand up slowly. A deer approaches on the far side of the thicket. Suddenly Sandy lowers her head down level with her shoulders and charges at it – surely not a wifely greeting? The other deer runs away. Through the thicket I catch the unmistakeable flick of a tail, so the intruder was a fallow and almost at once it appears in full view, a yearling with a male tassel and little roundels on its forehead where most would already have small antlers growing, late born then or a late developer, though sexually precocious enough, walking purposefully round where the does had been lying, smelling the ground and also the dead branches where they had left their scent. Did this mean the roe were coming on heat? They usually wait till the end of June at least, more often July. In any case, fallow bucks are not supposed to be interested in sex till September at the earliest and certainly not with roe!

When a fallow doe in dappled summer chestnut appears beside him, the yearling looks up. Both notice me beneath the oak, stand stock still for a moment with that affronted look, then gallop away. For a moment the glade is empty, but almost at once, Sandy roe trots lightly back. She goes without a glance to her favourite place behind the thicket and in her turn begins to smell around in a concerned sort of way everywhere the fallow has left his scent, finally doing a round of all the dead bough ends, rubbing her face and forehead against them, re-marking her territory with the scent gland just below the eyes. She takes no notice of me at all, though I have not moved since startling off the fallow, which does demonstrate what extraordinarily highly-strung animals they are.

Sandy roe in fact decides to amble across the clearing towards me. A few yards away she comes to a holly, frayed white low down by a male, and scrapes at the scar he has made with a hoof while marking his boundaries, then walks on to a birch which has a half-dead branch hanging off it at nose level. She sniffs the tip delicately and nibbles it. When she tries to rub her forehead against it, the twig jumps back, and she starts back too, eyes it askance, waits, peers forward, touches it lightly with her wet, black nose. When it springs away again, she goes wild, butts at it, scrapes with her forefeet, butts again, kicks up her heels, dances all round the tree, butts it again, pirouettes on her back legs, batting the twig with her front hooves, skipping sideways as cloud shadows chase across the glade and the jay flashes past with yet another beakful. Of all my deer-watching hours, in the forest, I would not have missed this for the world. Finally she kicks up her back legs twice, gives her play-twig a last nuzzle and moves away into the oaks.

I give her a moment, then creep after her, but there is no sign for a while. With the sunshine, a few butterflies have appeared, wood browns and large whites. The chaffinch chorus continues overhead till upset by a commotion higher up the slope, and there is Sandy roe running fast through the trees. It is afternoon now and she has probably been scared by walkers, but after a moment she skids to a halt and looks over her shoulder with an unmistakably feminine air. Another roe appears, catching her up – the buck. They gallop off, flying through the sunny glades and shady hollows far off, lost, then the crashing becomes louder and they are back again, circling round. For a moment both stop, ten yards apart. The buck tosses his antlers and they are off again, away and up through the trees to the north. Quiet returns to the wood and I wonder if I will see them again.

To the mere human mind, the roe deer year is most peculiarly organized, with all the excitement compressed into May and June. The buck chases away his last year's offspring, probably twins, driving them off to seek out territories of their own. The doe gives birth. The buck roams around establishing rights on new territory for himself, but returns to the old one to mate, books say in July, but in my forest it is often in June and by the present goings on, it will certainly be early this year. Even so, the doe's twins will not start to develop till late autumn because of delayed implantation, the same as in the badger. If my pair were merely going off to inspect new ground, wouldn't the buck lead the way? It is very difficult to think like a deer, but that chase was surely the beginning of courting, though it is only the end of May. So much to learn: I had no idea till this morning that female roe marked territory with their scent glands.

'Big ears, big ears!' the thrush was shouting when I came back to Swines a few days later; meanwhile the blackbird had perfected a convincing wolf whistle. Both were drowned out by the jay's scolding consternation when a crow ventured too near the oak tree nest. A little blob sunbathing on the end of a thorn twig turned out to be an infant coal tit, waiting to be fed. Moving down through the familiar series of glades in cool early sunlight, I spotted deer at once in the distance. Flitting between the oaks I soon realized it was a fallow. For once she did not notice me, peacefully grazed on. As I arrived on the edge of the roe's clearing, something moved under the far trees, and the yearling fallow strolled out into full view, a really weedy specimen, light coated but without the beautiful pale shine of the true menil. He walked confidently towards me, then sensed I was there and pronked comically away into cover.

Rain overnight had brought out little turf flowers in this low-lying part, tormentil and lousewort among the leathery green buttons of pennywort. The thrush was singing 'watch it, watch it!' but the hares paid no heed, pottering contentedly about the wood. A glimpse of deer movement and hopes rise that the roe have returned, but through the glasses I can see it is the two fallow does and the scrawny yearling already watching me with deep suspicion, then all of a sudden they take off at a gallop, running diagonally past me and up into the wood. This time there were four of them, perhaps the three fallow were being chased off by a roe. It is worth waiting to see if one returns, mission accomplished. I am hidden behind a self-seeded rhododendron which has just come into purple bloom and thrums with bees.

Nothing moves. Presently, having decided to work slowly along the deer fence to make sure – or as sure as one can – that the roe have really gone, I make a last sweep with the glasses and discover the fallow group has settled down to chew the cud halfway up the long slope of oak and beech. There are still four of them: the newcomer seems to have small antlers, perhaps a sorrel, though it is difficult to tell ages at this time of year when fallow antlers are only part grown. He is rather pale . . . sandy . . . in fact not a fallow at all but Sandy roe buck! I do refrain from singing and dancing, but am really glad he is still here, presumably with wife and kids. And what on earth is he doing, sitting there peacefully chewing the cud with *fallow*, upturning all the theories that roe bucks are fiercely possessive of territory and never associate with other deer?

Soon the fallow yearling stood up, followed by the other two and the three of them moved on up the slope, pausing to graze here and there, eventually disappearing from view. A few minutes later the roe buck stood up and moved downhill. Waiting to see if he would meet up with his family, I stalked him for a long time. Now and then he would pause to strip some ivy from an oak, or graze the edge of a clearing, but obviously his main purpose was to beat the bounds of his territory, scraping at the base of a small holly then stripping off more green bark where there were already white scars. At the dead tree by the fence, he spent a long time rubbing his face against the bare twig ends. Turning back into the wood, he made for the dead branch where I had seen the kid hiding and made a leisurely tour of all those twig ends as well, in fact he seemed obsessed with dead wood, seeking out every fallen tree or branch in the vicinity. Very little fraying or scraping went on, but a great deal of scent marking; altogether it was a day full of surprises. Head high, small, sharp antlers held with pride, he crossed an open glade in full sunshine. It took time to creep round the edge and I lost him, for that day.

I returned very early on a still, blue morning promising midsummer warmth to come. No other cars had yet parked, but while pulling on boots I heard a rustle behind me, out towards the road. There was no one there. The highest branches of the tallest beech hung utterly still in the humid air, yet the rustle came again, from a deserted stretch of gravel. If only George had been there he would have sorted it out at once: it took me several minutes to trace the culprit. In the middle of the car park, the Forestry Commission had provided a large roofed litter bin, tastefully constructed of rough logs, with two slots like a pillar box. From one of these a grey squirrel was looking out at the world as if from his own front door, then he disappeared into the depths of the bin and loud rustling began again. A light dew lay on the grass of the clearings, greying their green, but none of them betrayed deer tracks. The usual chaffinches were about and a green woodpecker looped past. A far glimpse of chestnut through the gloom beneath the oaks proved to be ponies. I walked slowly down to the favourite clearing, sat there for a long time, then tried to follow the maze of deer and pony paths through the bracken and foxgloves where the wood narrows, but there was no trace of deer. They could well be sitting there, watching me. I visited all the beloved bare branches: no sign. Guelder rose was just coming into flower, hanging out its creamy white panicles at the edge of a clearing. Soon the air was so heavy with heat, even the birds fell silent. The roe had vanished away.

It was July before I could return, but this was an interesting time for it could still be the roe rutting season. I had been practising a high 'pee-you' call, the cry of a maiden roe, said to bring bucks from far and near at this time. I had come to love this stretch of wood, each glade a secret room, its treasure unlocked only by stealth. Oak and beech boughs hung heavy and summer-dark. It was very early but already the air was alive with the whirrings of wood crickets, like tiny sewing machines. In the first glade a badger was just making a late way home, shuffling slowly across the grass, lowering his striped snout now and then to search for beetles, disturbing a little owl who screamed down at him then turned its head right round over its back to stare at me before gliding off. The second glade framed two fallow bucks with half-grown antlers, grazing side by side, but the third, the roe's favourite, was ringed with red and yellow plastic ribbon: a notice said DANGER KEEP OUT FELLING. Even while I stared at this, stunned, a yellow forwarder truck came roaring into sight from the opposite side.

So there was nothing for it but to try again further north, strange territory to me. The wood still sloped down, but much more steeply: the many tall trees blocked out the sun, and there was little grass, no open glades at all and everywhere treacherously crisp carpets of dry leaves. I tried walking barefoot but it was no quieter. The bottom of the slope seemed to be more open country and strewn with dead trees, so I slowly picked a way down to level ground. There was no fence here to limit the deer's range, instead a belt of small, self-seeded willow and birch thinned out onto marsh. There were no obvious signs, such as droppings or frays, yet I knew, with a shiver of excitement, that there were deer about. Chris Ferris, in her wonderful badger-watching books describes how she taught herself to see in the dark: hidden in us all, not quite totally atrophied, must be those extra senses possessed by our remote caveman ancestors, essential for living off the land.

The hurricane of 1987 seemed to have cut a swathe all along the foot of the slope, leaving dead trees lying at every angle. I chose a fallen beech as a good vantage point and walked towards it through waist-high bracken – and all but tread on a female roe which leaps up and bounds away and, even as I stare at her in delight, another, smaller roe jumps up too and follows, though only for a hundred yards, then both turn to size me up. I feel a real intruder, waking them up like that from their peaceful snooze. The second doe must be a yearling, another one that has not been chased away from the parents' territory.

I sit down on the beech trunk anyway to give them time to settle. Beyond it the ground slopes upward, thickly planted with young beech only some twenty feet high: a rustling makes me peer up through the slim sapling trunks. There, totally unconcerned at their elders' flight or my presence, two little roe kids are feeding on the moss. Each is about the size of a smallish fox, though almost tail-less, a deep foxy red, with enormous ears. Though they are merely grazing, their childish energy and high spirits are apparent. When one comes to a fallen twig, it jumps high over it as if on springs and now and then one barges into the other, accidently-on-purpose, as brothers will, for a friendly shove. I watch enchanted till they move away over the brow of the hill.

As I seemed to have stumbled on the heart of roe territory, I stayed on the beech trunk. Even deer cannot walk through those crisp leaves without a sound. A rustle high up the main bank betrayed another doe, with a black patch on her face and a single kid following close behind, larger than either of the twins. It was my ambition to see a whole family together, doe, buck and twins. A cloud of large white butterflies danced about the spaces of the wood. In its shade few flowers bloomed for them, only the straggly white spikes of enchanter's nightshade with a scatter of tormentil and cow-wheat. Doe and kid wandered slowly out of sight. For a long time nothing moved till a crashing high up revealed a buck with poor antlers hurrying away south. Had I seen all the family now, though separately? A good half mile separated the two car park entrances to Swines, so the long stretch of wood between could be hiding whole families.

It was tempting to set off south at once, but I stayed put on my beech and, sure enough, before evening the tall ferns to my left silently parted and a fine roe buck strolled up into the plantation, beginning to graze on the silvery green tumps of bun moss. With a deep red coat, bright buff rump patch and strong antlers with three points on each side, he was a buck in his prime. I was anxious to try out my 'pee-you' call, but afraid of disturbing him. As I watched him ambling through the slim trunks, I realized there were two deer: a doe had materialized by his side in that uncanny way, not the one with a black face patch, so perhaps the twins' mother.

Through the willow scrub in the valley bottom came a constant flicker of orange, probably a hatch of fritillaries; a tree creeper glided up the nearest beech, pausing to probe the bark with its small curved beak, and a plump squirrel came to a fallen birch close by, sitting bolt upright in profile, turning and turning one of last year's nuts in his paws. Then a loud squeak recalled me to the plantation. One of the roe kids came hurtling down over the brow of the hill, closely followed by twin. With another squeak he skidded to a halt beside his mother, butted her udder vigorously, and began to suck. The buck never glanced up from grazing though he was only a few yards away. So here at last was the whole roe family together, many weeks after I had left the mouth of Buckland Water.

Walking homeward up the steep slope, I caught sight of roe-colour further along, but could not make sense of it, unless the deer was up in the air! Through the glasses it certainly proved to be a deer, for it moved slightly, but still seemed mysteriously high, half hidden by the massive boles of tall beeches, so I set out to stalk it as quietly as the dead leaves would allow, first along the valley bottom through the line of dead trees where there was a little grass, then up the bank. The rufous patch twitched from time to time but did not move away.

I had expected the roe family to be my abiding memory of Swines Wood, but there was another. A huge old beech had snapped off some ten feet from the ground: its fall had caused the hollow trunk to break asunder, like a canoe tipped up at an angle though miraculously some of the branches were alive and in bright leaf. And high in his canoe reclined a roe buck: he gave me a haughty glance down that straight nose, then his eyelids drooped in the warm evening sunshine. All around the shattered tree danced a cloud of brilliant amber pearl-washed fritillaries, so bright and perfect they must only have hatched that day. One lighted on the buck's head, but he merely twitched an ear. I could see by the small antlers that he was probably the yearling I had seen earlier. Arrogant and handsome on his high couch among the butterflies, he could have been some heraldic beast from the dawn of the world.

Really going home now, with nothing to lose, I slid behind an oak, waited a few minutes, then called 'pee-you, pee-you'. After all, what could be more exciting to a young buck than the call of a virgin doe?

'Pee-you, pee-you!'

Eagerly I peered round the tree. Young buck vouchsafed me one bored glance, then slowly closed his eyes . . .

FENNY CROSS

I STAMPED on the brakes so hard the car skidded on the loose gravel, but the little creature reached the verge safely and vanished into a dark wood of conifers, their branches sighing under the stars. What was it?

Till now it had been a disappointing evening; I had come to Fenny Cross to look for sika deer. Fenny is a range of mixed woodland, some of it pine plantations, sloping north, criss-crossed by gravel forestry tracks, dipping down to a vast stretch of wet bogland and heath, in season the home of Dartford warblers, nesting snipe and rare orchids. The sika live in this belt of woods, seldom crossing bog to the north or road to the south. Because you were fairly certain of seeing them here, sika lacked for me the magical, elusive quality of fallow or roe, so I had put off looking for them. Also sika watching was easy, no hours of stalking or patient lying in the bracken being munched by insects – theoretically you simply drove down a track and waited, using the car as a hide.

So, with half an hour of daylight to spare, I had parked at a crossroads where they always emerged at dusk to graze on the wide verges of hummocky grass, pitted with puddles, dotted with seedling pines and fringed by huge old pollarded oaks. As dusk began to fall a goldcrest sang its high tinkling song from the nearest pine. A faint rustle overhead and a flock of long-tailed tits landed on an oak: for a moment the darkening air was full of their sweet, tissy-tissy twitters, then off they flew again, little flecks of black and white. The wood beyond the fence was close-planted young oak and beech with a few rogue fir and birch; the beech still retained some of their old dead leaves that rustled in the chill February air, but nothing else moved. I waited till a small moon shone down through the great oak boughs, then turned for home, driving slowly, still hoping for a sight of the sika.

Then this spaniel-sized, auburn-coloured deer ran straight out of the woods and across the track. I waited a long time, but no other deer appeared. As sika hinds bear their calves in June, this year's young would be three-quarters grown by now and surely in the same dun winter coats as their parents? Could this possibly have been a muntjac? One had been spotted in the forest years before, by my friend Barbara, but I had never seen one here.

Muntjac from India and China were introduced into various parks including Woburn and Whipsnade early this century. Escapees bred successfully, so there is now a scattered wild population living here and there in Britain in woods with thick undergrowth. They are about twenty-one inches tall at the shoulder, even smaller than roe, a foxy colour with an arched back and very short spiky antlers. I had not noticed any antlers, but then the little creature had disappeared so quickly; certainly it left an impression of a humped back. It would be very exciting if muntjac were returning to the forest.

So next day I returned with Barbara. We decided not to walk through the woods in daylight and risk disturbing any deer, but gave George a run out on the heath, then parked on the verge of the track near last night's sighting, arriving again in daylight so all would be quiet by dusk. George stretched himself along the shelf under the back window, and peered into the trees.

We knew little about muntjac behaviour, just hoped they might be creatures of habit like the sika and fallow. A robin sang out from the nearest oak, but flew off, disturbed by a Land Rover towing a horsebox which came too fast down the rough track and stopped just beyond us. A woman jumped out, ran to my window and shouted, 'Have you seen any pigs?' No, we had not: it seemed late in the season for pigs still to be on the forest (they are sent out in the autumn to fatten up on the acorn crop). She ran back and opened the horsebox. Out jumped three children and four assorted dogs. They all gambolled away into the woods with loud barks and shrill cries of 'Coop, coop,' crashing through the undergrowth and waking a hundred woodpigeons from their high roosts. There would be no deer that night.

But the next evening, no sooner had I parked than several sika appeared nonchalantly feeding just inside the wire strand fence, with a thrush still singing high in an oak in the day's last wintry sunshine, so the light was good enough to see them well. The nearest hind was the dull grey-brown of winter fallow, with a gingery tinge to the head and a dark streak running down the neck from between the ears. The easiest way to differentiate them from fallow (since they are roughly the same size) is by general shape – the sika is much more barrel-bodied, lacking the fallow's elegance of line. Nevertheless it was delightful to see them at last, ambling peacefully about the wood's edge, nibbling at fallen branches and mossy roots.

When another hind joined the group, she came face to face with one already grazing that spot. They both reared up and executed a sort of waltz turn, though this appeared to be a friendly enough greeting, as they then fell to grazing side by side. The next newcomer was met by brief knuckling of foreheads together. The first hind to come level with the car stopped grazing to stare at it, jaws still working. She stared for a full minute; George stared back; then she returned to eating moss. As twilight began to fall, first one then all the herd ducked under the fence to spread out over the grass verge ten yards away. Among the dozen animals, five were a little shorter and more slightly built than the rest: these must be last year's young ones.

As the moon shone down through the oak's ancient boughs, silvering the sika's pale underparts, they decided to cross the track. As each one reached the middle, she paused and stared at the car, then walked on, white rump disappearing into the moon-striped western woods.

But of my little deer-mystery, there was no sign at all. We must come again.

The next evening, grey and rainy, not a single deer appeared. A lone heron flapped ponderously by, heading for the bog where

frogs might be on the way to mating pools; nothing else moved; sika might never have existed at Fenny Cross. A hundred years ago they certainly did not, for, compared with red and fallow, they are mere interlopers. Two had escaped from a nearby estate herd early this century, shortly joined by two more. All the sika in these woods are thought to be descended from that four, though originally the breed came from China, imported in the nineteenth century to ornament large grounds or provide extra hunting.

Two days later, the rain a fine mist now, I came back and soon there were little movements inside the wood, flicks of tail and ear, a glimpse of white rump. Some half a dozen sika had ducked under the fence to graze on the verge for there was little feed left in the woods now except for moss. Ten minutes later came one more hind – and with her was my foxy-coloured little one.

It was obvious at once that he was not a muntjac, but a very late born sika, for he kept unusually close to his mother; wherever she went, his head stayed level with her hindquarters, almost huddling against her at times, not sucking, but lowering his head now and then to nibble the grass. They came quite close so that I could see the curiously humped back which had first made me think him a muntjac. Sika, like red and roe, have straight backs, even when young. Ten yards away, mother lifted her head to stare fixedly at the car, which was mud-coloured and muddy, but its real camouflage value was in masking the smell of dog and human. Keepers' vans used the forestry track all year, so the deer were used to the odd whiff of petrol, oil, hot metal. Baby never looked up, intent on staying confidingly close to mother, a small auburn shape against her dark coat in the misty twilight.

I guessed he must have been born around the turn of the year rather than the normal midsummer, a great disadvantage. Would he survive? Determined to watch his progress I came back to Fenny Cross many times, but never saw him again. In fact that was his last twilight. The keeper told me some time later that he had shot a young sika the very next day since he was an obvious weakling unlikely to make the spring.

Of course deer have to be culled, both to save them suffering and to prevent a population explosion which could only result in many starving; just the same, I could not help feeling sad for the little creature who had followed his mother so trustingly with those big dark eyes. The best way to banish his forlorn image would be to return later in the year and watch healthy young calves in the summer woods, so it was June when I returned.

Far down through the wood a shadow fell on a tree trunk – and was gone. Something pale flitted into sight and vanished: a distant twig cracked; dead leaves rustled momentarily; light fell on a dead branch in shadow before; one leaf of bracken moved, for no reason. Maybe there were deer strolling about in the depths of the wood, or was it the edge of a pigeon's wing, a breeze-caught frond of fern or a butterfly waking to the sun? All day I searched the pine woods and their grassy rides, the only movement small orange gatekeepers flickering over tormentil and self-heal growing along the verges; not a trace of deer. Warm sun drew a lovely fragrance from the trees and once a family of goldfinches flew by crying, 'tuee, tuee.'

Towards evening, following a runnel out of the woods, I came to a pond which was sometimes used by the stags as a wallow in the rutting season. Many hoofprints slotted the mud, but they were old, with no sign of droppings. Spearwort fringed the pond, amongst it the lilac whorls of water mint, pink flowering rush and the velvet brown spikes of half-grown great reed mace. Further along the wood's edge, a whole stretch glowed purple-pink with rosebay willowherb just coming into bloom, a perfect setting for young sika, but empty.

Back in the car with dusk falling, tired, reaching for the thermos, something made me glance up into the driving mirror. Crossing the gravel track was a sika hind with a skittish little rufous brown calf, straight backed and happy to prance away from his mother – then they were gone into the darkening woods; so I had a snapshot at least, if not a picture, to banish the image of my winter waif.

Earlier in the year, towards the end of May, I had spent an afternoon here with Steve Smith who has been studying sika for many years and spends all his spare time out here watching them. Tall foxgloves fringed the rides: the deer had even spared a patch of pale, heath spotted orchids in a ditch. Turning a corner we came upon a little group of sika hinds, one still in shabby mouse-brown winter coat, one in smooth summer chestnut and a third patched half and half. Steve knew them all individually.

We searched in the bracken along the narrowest grass rides where they most often drop their young, since it was just possible a calf had been born that early, but all we found was a comfortable couch of pressed-down fern where a doe or hind had lain to chew the cud, and several other little groups of sika still placidly grazing together, so used to Steve they hardly glanced up.

A single, spotted fallow did bound off toward the trees in the usual nervy way. After the strange goings on in Swines Wood between fallow and roe, I asked him about relations between fallow and sika, but he had never seen them play or fight together, only graze sedately within sight of each other. Just then a young squirrel swung right across the ride in front of us, so it was just as well that

George had been left behind – dogs were not Steve's favourite animal. The previous year a labrador had chased two pregnant hinds for several hours, chivvying them all round these pine woods: afterwards both gave birth to dead calves. There is in fact a 'Dogs on leads' notice on every gate, with a clear symbol of a leashed dog for those who cannot read . . .

Another grim time came just before Christmas, Steve said, when gangs of poachers descended on Fenny Cross with dazzle lamps, lurcher dogs and silenced rifles in the darkest hours of the night when no one is about. If you are offered venison at a peculiarly reasonable price, ask yourself why: better still, ask the vendor.

Walking back to Steve's car we looked in vain for the wallaby said to have escaped from a nearby park and taken refuge here. We discussed whether they should release a female to keep him company: after all, wallabies live happily enough in the wild in Staffordshire, but had to admit a breeding colony would be one more pressure on the already overgrazed forest.

Steve then showed me his splendid collection of photographs, which included a lost looking sika calf gazing up into the face of a stag, several fallow swimming in a pool and a sika stag rolling in his favourite mud-wallow. He also had a fine pair of sika antlers, the two branches picked up entire and uneaten within a few yards of each other. These are like red deer antlers, though smaller, always round in section; this pair had come from an eight-pointer, that is, with four points on each side, so a stag in his prime – only occasionally do sika grow ten points. Deer are said to eat their antlers for their calcium content.

'So where are all the stags?' I asked.

Steve said that after the rut they tended to disappear from this part of the forest. I wondered about this after we had said goodbye. While I had been with him, the sika had taken little notice of me, but now, when I came round a bend surprising a solitary hind, she leapt away at once, affronted, expanding her rump patch into a big white powder puff as sika do in their comical way when alarmed.

If the stags were not in this part of Fenny Cross, where were they? Since they like tree cover, the herd would hardly choose the boglands and heath to the north, but beyond both lay Moon Hill, covered with oak, beech and a scatter of dark yew. Might the sika be lying up there?

So next day George and I set out across the heath. Along its edge stood a row of hawthorn, five of them, identically pruned into curious milk-churn shapes by browsing deer. A flock of tree pippits flew out of them, though a willow warbler went on with his sweet, light song. Small concrete platforms lay half embedded in the turf, relics of a war-time searchlight camp. This sounds like a horrid intrusion into the landscape, but nature has long since reclaimed them for her own. One is just like a large golden hearth rug, square cornered, so thickly is it covered with the starry flowers of biting stone crop. Another which detained us longer was red with wild strawberries, hundreds of perfect, ripe little berries deliciously sharp-sweet. George likes blackberries but found these a little tart.

Though too early for the real heather display, tufts of cross-leaved heath were showing pink among the russet of shepherd's sorrel and heath bedstraw. Small heath butterflies fluttered about the flowers, seldom pitching, and one beautiful pale buff, furry fox moth, sitting on the heather vibrating its wings to generate energy for take-off. Further out, gorse thickets took over, habitat of the rare Dartford warbler which spends much of its time hunting for spiders among the rough stems or perching on the tops. Sure enough, some distance away were three thickets, each with a small bird on the topmost twig, silhouetted against the grey sky, but almost at once, a 'chink-chink' alarm cry like two pebbles knocked together betrayed that these were stone chats.

Soon the male, with his darker brown head and brighter orange breast with touches of white, flew over to the next bush and displayed before the more sober female, fanning his wings and dancing on the air like a humming bird. The female flicked her tail and flew away, unimpressed. As we passed by, several stone chats changed bushes with loud 'chink-chinks'. Further away more little birds posed on top twigs, but it was a grey day, dulling wing colours so they looked like uniform dark cut-outs. I had in fact chosen this cool morning for George's sake. It can be blazingly hot out here without a trace of shade; that is when the adders are at their most active. I always wear boots in the forest, but the dachshund figure seems particularly vulnerable.

From a distance the heather plain looked dull and featureless, yet the bushes hid all sorts of treasures, a single tall white butterfly orchid, spiky yellow pettywhin and that tiny green, fern-like plant, moonwort. George flushed a pair of partridges which ran away, leaving three fledglings behind, dumpy little speckled things,

pecking unconcerned about the grass. Northward a curlew uttered its lonely, bubbling cry; we were walking downhill towards the great spread of bog.

All along its edge ran a wide stretch of good grass, rather like the lawns beside forest rivers, and here ponies had congregated, many with foals. One was grooming its mother while she grazed, two leggy little chestnut ones lay flat out on the grass feigning death in their splendidly relaxed way, a darker one sucked its mother till she stamped with annoyance, then went back to grazing. A bay mare and a grey stood in silent communion, forehead to forehead. George ignored even the most skittish in his gentlemanly way, moreover I had thrown down the haversack, which must mean a picnic. But we never had it. Walking north I had been vaguely aware that the light had grown gloomier, leaching colour from the land. Turning to find a patch of grass free of pony droppings, I saw why.

Out of the south-west had risen up a monstrous iron-grey cloud, black in its folds, which towered over the heath like a huge dark hand, the height of it toppling forward as if the hand reached out – for us. I stared at it, mesmerized, at once reminded of how Wordsworth had come upon a dark mountain peak which seemed to threaten him personally, the night he stole a boat ('The Prelude'):

> And growing still in stature the grim shape
> Towered up between me and the stars, and still
> For so it seemed, with purpose of its own
> And measured motion like a living thing,
> Strode after me.

Even as I watched, the blackness was rent by lightning. Wordsworth had rowed swiftly back; George and I set off at a steady lope – the wide heath was no place to be caught in a thunderstorm.

Because the fallow breeding season intervened, it was in fact August before I could return to the quest for sika stags, the heath now in full summer splendour, spreading away in rolling purple acres on every side and a-hum with bees. Pausing to look for the showy emerald caterpillars of the emperor moth, I came upon a bare hollow where an adder basked in the sun, strategically laid out in a loose hank, like a skein of wool, on the north side for maximum warmth, reddish brown beneath the black zigzags, so probably a young one, head narrower than its body, tiny eyes watching me. Later another whipped into the heather as I passed; George had stayed prudently at home.

Out on the bog, silvery bog pimpernel leaves trailed over spongy sphagnum, sundew had put up small white flowers, the showiest were the gold starred spikes of asphodel. In a previous year I had found sky blue gentians close by and in the wettest, stinking pools, bog orchid, an inconspicuous little yellow knob, exciting only for its rarity.

Where the land rose towards the woods of Moon Hill grew bushes of bog myrtle, smelling of resin and balsam in the warm sun, covered with yellow pompoms like a tiny mimosa. Heather took over the drier slopes, now busy with butterflies, mostly little silver-studded blues. And here at last were deer tracks. Even printed clearly in black on a white page, there is not a great deal to differentiate hoofprints. A sika stag's slot is half a centimetre longer than a red hind's, half a centimetre shorter than a fallow buck's and slightly slimmer and more pointed than either. Translate this onto trampled mud and it is very difficult to read, but I followed the tracks hopefully between tall birches into the shade of Moon Hill, where beeches stretched away up the slope, wide spread, stately old trees with soaring silver grey trunks, their heavy summer canopy shading a floor of old leaves and bracken. Nothing moved; no birds sang. I followed the narrow trodden pathway up through the trees with quickening excitement at the sight of droppings, shiny and fresh. Surely this must be the sika stags' summer hiding place?

Nearing the top of the rise, I dropped on all fours, moved very slowly, reached the base of a huge bole on the summit, peered carefully round – and froze. Halfway down the north slope, an antler rose above the fern. Silently standing up, edging round the trunk, gazing through binoculars, I saw them, a herd of maybe twenty male deer lying down in a hollow among the bracken with their backs to me, peacefully chewing the cud together, each one bearing antlers according to his age – and every one a fallow.

Moving east brought them into full view: I was looking down on their dappled backs, though they were sitting so close together their antlers seemed almost entwined. Where the sun broke through high leaves to shine directly upon them, the antlers looked pink, for they were still in velvet. Presently, as the sun rose higher, the bucks began to stand up, one by one and move off downhill at a dignified pace, spreading out at the wood's edge, beginning to graze, so at

last it was possible to view them as individuals and see the variety of antler patterns: if one stayed long enough with this herd, it would be possible to recognize each buck easily by his antlers.

The one nearest to me had oversized brow-tines, the forward facing points just above the forehead. Next came the king of them all with immense antlers palmated (flattened out) to twice the width of my hand, spread like great branches. Next to him grazed another with equal palmations but curving inward at the top so that their tips were only a foot apart. Of the oldest bucks, one was very dark with a black face and very tall but spindly brown antlers. Two others bore almost identical pairs, high and narrow, but spreading into wide Japanese fan shapes at the top. The buck nearer to me had a deep V-shaped division in its left fan, which must have been some deformity in its growth, for the velvet was not damaged.

After these came antlers of younger deer, some quite tall but scarcely palmated, down to a buck in his second antlered year with two points on each side, but none with the simple V shape of a pricket – perhaps they had all stayed with their mothers. Pottering peacefully in and out of shadow at the wood's edge, with three magpies pecking about between their hooves and an amber fritillary passing by, they made a beautiful picture in their dappled chestnut coats, though soon they would be going through the irritating and untidy business of shedding their velvet, the oldest first.

A cloud of chaffinches flew in, bringing the beeches alive with their fussing and twittering. One by one, the bucks kneeled down, apparently at random, yet when all were resting once again, the extended herd had become a close-knit group, flank touching flank. Black face chewed his cud, but the drowsy summer air was too much, eyes began to close, head to nod; but the weight of antlers drew his head backwards. Three times a tine touched his back and he awoke abruptly, balanced his head again, but the fourth time gave in and stretched right out, chin on the ground. A magpie alighted on his rump, but he never twitched. The rest of the herd were similarly drowsing off, only the youngest with less weight to carry went on chewing their cud, heads erect, gazing out over the flat bogland to the purple heath. Chaffinches flew away, the magpies too; eyelids drooped, a summer hum of insects filling the still air. Then, onto this drowsy scene skipped a fawn, tiny beside the great-antlered bucks. He ran at full stretch past the herd, uphill, heading east. None of them gave him so much as a glance.

Fallow buck are supposed to form herds away from females but two hundred yards from them a group of does grazed among bracken in a clearing where a huge beech had fallen. Two fawns on 'solids' were already eating the grass, though still with blunt puppy-heads and coats paler than their mothers' rich chestnut. So Moon Hill was full of fallow, but of a sika stag there was no sign. I must wait till September when the rutting season would draw them irresistibly back to the woods of Fenny Cross. All this was obviously a judgement upon me for thinking sika predictable.

October: the great oaks tinged with mustard yellow above carpets of brown acorns, a necklace of scarlet briony winding round a fence post, a chill evening mist creeping up from the bog to the north and only a squirrel moves, racing across the gravel track. Exactly at six o'clock a sika stag trots out of the pines; by now the mist is a strange, dense white layer covering the ground so that the stag appears only as a pair of disembodied antlers gliding above it and vanishes into the woods opposite.

The next evening promised to be clear. I was on watch by five o'clock, listening for distant calls. Under the nearest oak a squirrel dug frantically for an acorn though they lay strewn all round him on the ground; he sat up and began to eat, but another squirrel suddenly appeared from behind the trunk and they chased off up into the boughs; the evening air drifted with the bitter pungent smell of raked-up leaves. A faint rustling falls on the still air, a quiet hoof-step . . .

Exactly at six o'clock a small group of sika appears from just inside the fence, grazes about on scattered tumps of moss, then one by one duck under the wire and wander out to graze on the wide verges beneath the oaks, only some ten yards away, in full view, with another half hour's daylight. First comes a big dark stag, barrel-bodied, then a hind with her young one, closely followed by another stag with slightly smaller antlers – just the situation for a fight. Rustlings still sound from the eastern woods so there are more to come probably. Another hind ducks under the fence, but at that moment a Land Rover inscribed Royal Navy roars down the track and halts in front of me, churning gravel. Chaps jump out and shout importantly about map references and ETAs above the noise of the engine.

When they shot off again, the sika had of course melted away into the shadowy pines. A little owl alighted silently on the nearest oak and screamed 'kee-o' three times. I felt like joining in.

Next day it seemed a good idea to get away from the car hide on this too accessible road and walk through the woods, though walking here is restricted to a ruler-straight gravel track. A few rogue birch and mountain ash drooping scarlet berries have been allowed to fringe the verges, otherwise the regimented pines are broken into blocks by wide grass fire breaks intersected by ditches. Sprigs of ragwort still bloomed along the ride with a few late thistles and even one purple spike of foxglove.

On the first strip of grass grazed three hinds, faces a paler brown than their winter coats. As I moved slowly past they raised their heads to stare, but made no move to run away, so less nervy than the fallow. At the next, two stags leapt up from the grass, taken by surprise. They ran only a few yards, then stopped to stare back indignantly. The larger one barked once, then trotted away into the trees and returned chivvying a hind in front of him with his spindly antlers — some sign of the rut at last. His neck showed the temporary thickening typical of stags in the rutting season, but there were still no mating cries; the hind stared at him for a moment, decided he wouldn't do, walked over to the smaller stag and they moved off together under the trees. Shouldn't there be screams of rage and clashings of antler? The bigger stag fell to grazing . . . The hinds could not be in season yet. Best wait a few days.

So it was the last Friday in October when we returned, George on the parcel shelf. A golden autumn afternoon had the grey squirrels in a frenzy of activity, six or seven were in sight at once, all young ones. Whilst waiting for sunset I decided to watch one and try to discern any pattern in its behaviour.

It ran across the track, grabbed up an acorn, sat down to eat it under one of the giant oaks, then flew along a row of dead branches, three feet off the ground, dashed up a small holly, peered into a hole, came down again, shot eight feet up an oak, paused to have a swearing match with another young squirrel climbing an adjacent tree, with much shaking of tails, came down again, dug a hole fast and buried an acorn, climbed up and up the nearest oak and swung away through the yellowing leaves out of sight. It is very difficult to follow the wonderfully inconsequent squirrel mind.

Meanwhile, exciting rustles and footfalls came from the darkening pines: slow and cautious little sounds quite different from the frantic scampers of squirrels, or blackbirds fossicking on the forest floor. A stag walked out of the wood, stood posed and noble, antlers high, in the middle of the track, lifted his head, gasped, then gave a high-pitched scream. As if this were a signal, sika streamed out on to the grass verge, hinds, stags and calves. Another stag cried out, bringing an admonitory growl from the parcel shelf. (Considering that my singing causes him to howl like a wolf, George was being remarkably restrained.) Soon there were dark bodies all round the car, whistling, grunting, bleating: sometimes a stag would run a few yards after a hind and once two stags reared up at one another, but most of the time they stood still, shaking the gathering twilight with their haunting banshee calls.

GOOSE LAKE

A T FIRST, the only life among the mats of broken-down old reed stems seemed to be the six-inch sprouts of yellow iris leaves, then there came a single, betraying croak – at least that is the usual name for a toad's utterance. This, though, was a gentle, wistful sound, like the plucking of a single harp string. Two or three times it came, while I searched and at last caught the glint of a golden eyelid. Four heads were poking out of the water just to eye level, two belonging to female toads with smaller males clinging to their backs. One of the pairs looked really comic. An enormous, knobby, prehistoric looking creature with a warty skin brindled pink and brown had sky blue 'eyebrows', and a tiny greeny yellow male clasped round her neck, like a jockey on a shire horse!

It is the single toads with their heads out of the water to the neck who are making the piping sounds; their flanks heave and bodies jerk forward with each note. They vary in colour from fawn with black spots to dark brown to almost yellow. There must be a fair balance of sexes here, since none of those obscene looking footballs are visible when a dozen males are all trying to mate with one female. One solitary who had been chirping hopefully for half an hour and watching a motionless pair mating, suddenly saw a single toad appear on the bank. At once he slithered across the brown stems and threw an arm across its shoulders, which was at once shrugged off. He sat and thought for a bit, then attempted an embrace from the front. The lone toad, who was small and most likely another male, appeared to bite him in the throat and he shot off into deep water with strong kicks of the back legs.

One pair had been together for more than a hour, both with eyes closed; at last the male slid off and immediately another, who had been wistfully croaking all this time, swam up and attempted to take his place. But enough is enough: the female turned and gave him a quick kick in the belly which sent him sprawling into the water where he lay spraddled as if dead, stunned at such a reception.

During the mating session, two or three small frogs crossed to the water, very slim and svelte compared with the baggy toads, each with a line down the flank, like darts shaping a coat to a better fit: they were probably last year's tadpoles and too young to breed. But the toad population was obviously set to expand – long shining ropes of eggs hung from each mating female; every now and then one would paddle her back legs, making ripples which would coil the jelly trails around the water plants below.

I had really come to Goose Pool to watch for fallow coming down to drink, or even to swim. On returning three days later, blue eyebrows was still clasped by her yellow green lover – and three days later still. Had they unclasped in between or is this a world record?

Goose Lake is a beautiful tree-hung pool roughly shaped like a boomerang, half a mile from end to end, with beds of reeds, iris, giant reed mace and scrub willow, all splendid cover for birds. On this late March day, rooks cawed from the pines above and the new leaves of willow hazed the banks with tender green all round the shining level of this well named lake, for, out on the water, two Canada geese were courting, facing one another, arching their long black necks and dabbling their bills, white cheek patches shining in the sun. When another goose swam too close, they drove him off with great flappings of powerful wings, indignant shaking of tails and high calls.

Further out, two great crested grebes were diving, then they too broke off and swam along very close, side by side in full spring plumage of chestnut ruffs and dark ear tufts. The male spent a long

time preening his breast feathers, while the female tried out a scuttle along the surface; pair bonding seemed to be in only the preliminary stages for presently they drifted apart and began to dive, staying under for about twenty seconds; today I was not to see their spectacular dancing on the water display. A moorhen pirruped deep in the reeds, a pair of coot pottered along the shore line, reed bunting chased about the willows and a high clamour of geese came from higher up the reach.

Returning in April, I found many deer slots by the lake where fallow had come down to drink, maybe to swim. I longed to see this. Last year there was rumour of a single fallow swimming across the Solent, from the New Forest to the Isle of Wight, and certainly sika are known to have swum ashore in Dorset from Brownsea Island. This day there were no deer, even on land, but Goose Pool was lively enough. The male reed bunting, smart in his black head feathers and white collar, flew constantly past with trails of grass several times his own length; out on the water the grebes were performing their comic courting display, teetering along on the surface, heads up, erect as guardsmen and oblivious of watchers, while in the reed bed, secretive coot crept silently about their domestic duties.

One swam past, scrambled quietly into the bed, found a platform of last year's stems, climbed carefully onto it and began to pull more stems down all round the edge to make her nest, constantly turning, weaving and treading it all down firmly. A second coot joined her, pulled down more stems and offered them to her; they worked peacefully together until the appearance of a third coot caused a flurry of wings all round and muted squawks. It appeared that number three had returned to the wrong nest, for she backed off at once and found her own some four feet away at a slightly higher level. Here she settled down, clicking her beak; her nest seemed to be finished. Made of dead reed stems in a forest of dead reeds, the nests are so well camouflaged it is impossible to see them when the birds are off.

A heron flew over, while another stood motionless, fishing on the far bank. A pair of jackdaws nesting in a half hollow oak close by, flew to and fro with maximum noise and squabble. (You could imagine the coot saying, 'We keep ourselves to ourselves.') A raft of shelduck floated past in their handsome green, white and chestnut, but all were upstaged by the geese.

A loud smack-smack and a pair of Canadas were running on the water with their big black webbed feet, then taking off for a nuptial flight right round the lake with lovely trumpeting cries, wings in synchronized beats; they landed back on the water exactly together, faced each other, bobbed heads, then drifted apart, tired after all the effort, till a second pair started off, then the third, so the first mounted up again, smacking over the lake; it was alive with ripples breaking the light and the wild honking of geese. When they returned to bob heads, a fourth pair took off. Out of sight over the woods, they obviously had a tiff, for one returned alone, flew a half circuit of the lake very low, and landed with no one to bob heads with. A flight of three arrowed across, but silently – perhaps a fishing party heading for the distant sea.

As no deer had come to drink, I decided to walk up through the woods to the Castle, the shore path first taking me past a rookery. These birds used to nest in a long avenue of elms nearby; when every tree succumbed to Dutch elm disease and was eventually felled, the birds took over a long straggle of pines along the north shore. In winter they sail back to roost here in clouds that darken the setting sun. Today nesting is in full swing. It looks like total chaos. Hundreds of birds are swirling round the pines, cawing, flapping their tattered looking wings and snatching twigs from each other. It seems amazing that chicks are actually reared in those tatty looking bundles of twigs.

Isolate a nest, watch through glasses, and a method does become obvious. Some birds are sitting tight on eggs; others are flying in with food, probably leather jackets or beetles. A few who are not nesting at all nevertheless defend their favourite branch with loud caws and aggressive open beak displays. Some birds are still flying in with nest material, twigs of willow or chestnut with new leaves, which they have broken off specially. One bird fancies the twig just brought in to another nest, sidles over and grabs it in his beak. 'Caw caw caw!' Deep rook consternation breaks out overhead.

A few youngsters already fledged balance on nest rims flapping their wings to strengthen them, constantly begging to be fed, leaning far forward with a gurgling sound, beak so wide open the bird appears to be about to vomit, revealing a startling red mouth. Parents changing shifts at the nest do so with comparatively little fuss, often quite silently, but the level of noise all round is really loud. Among the predominant cawings are various other cries, including a gutteral croak and a single really musical note, quite high pitched.

Last year a summer gale brought down one of the nests whole, so that it was possible to examine it. What from afar looked like a random bundle of twigs was in fact a cunningly constructed basket; presumably rooks break off green twigs because they are supple enough to weave in and out. Most surprising of all was its lining, a soft grass cup, elegantly crafted by those uncouth-looking beaks. As I walked on, every rook fell into the air cawing loudly, the racket dying away slowly behind me.

The Castle is a much loved place. I am Lady of the Castle, may sweep in at the main gate and stride its ramparts by the hour, for no one else ever seems to come here. There are no Norman towers or Tudor battlements for visitors to stare at, only a mossy bank bright with violets, inch-high wood sorrel and scattered celandines enclosing an oval of scattered trees, a larch in its first soft green, oaks in gold-green bud, birches hung with small catkins. A gap in the bank is the entrance or perhaps a mistake by a forestry tractor. Beside it stands a crab apple in bright pink blossom. Far more impressive 'castles' sail by in the blue April sky, great towers of white cumulus, but on such a morning I would not change this domain for Windsor itself or the heights of Edinburgh. Great tits fly to and fro exploring the older trees' mantle of ivy for nesting sites. This stops short at a browse line five feet above the ground, for the Castle's cohorts are its fallow deer.

I settle down to wait, my back against the broken bank at its highest point on the slope; chaffinches peck about the sunny forest floor, scattering briefly when a magpie lands overhead with its harsh, scolding rattle. The banks are so old, no one really knows who built them or why, but once, maybe two and a half thousand years ago, a whole gang of people must have worked here day after day, digging out a deep ditch and throwing up an earth wall, far higher then, to protect themselves and their beasts from some maurauding enemy. Had they cleared some acres of forest for crops, or did they simply run cattle on it, as the commoners do to this day?

A menil doe with her male yearling trot silently through the entrance, stare round for a moment, the sun shining pink through their ears, then fall to grazing. The faint breeze from the west is blowing in my face, so they work steadily towards me, seemingly oblivious. There is really little nutritious greenery here, and far better grass along the rides passing north and west, yet something seems to draw deer within these banks. When they are ten feet away, the young one sees – or smells – me, freezes, stares, so that I have a good view of his antler bumps, then leaps into the air and pronks off with mother, though only to the far end.

While tits and finches fly urgently past with trails of nesting material and foxes will be out all day hunting to feed their cubs, spring is a calm period with fallow, the rut long over, fawns not due till June, so it is interesting to see what social groups they form when not biologically driven. Just as mother and son disappeared from view, a small herd entered; mostly they do use the entrance though they could easily clear the bank with a bound. These did not pause to graze, but wandered slowly past, three does, two yearlings, a two-year-old buck with light antlers not palmated yet and one mature buck with tall antlers, palmated but not yet in their prime – they would both lose them soon.

Presently I stood up to leave, moving across the long shadowed floor towards the gap. Then it was my turn to freeze. A large herd was grazing the ride outside, ten or twelve does with some yearlings and, in the middle of them, a pure white doe, so beautiful among all the shabby old dark winter coats. Further along grazed a sandy coloured yearling who would gradually become white like her mother. I was delighted to find these two, not just for the look of them. From a practical point of view they would act as markers, making it easier to identify the herd again. If the young one stayed, it would be possible to check at what stage of coat moult she became pure white.

They were not staying long now. I had a fine view of white, heart-shaped rumps and switching tails keeping off the evening flies as they grazed slowly uphill, ambling about, pausing for a bite, a picture of content till suddenly every head went up, ears tall; in two seconds they had veered off into the northern woods and vanished away. I never did see what startled them. Later, a thin, rangy fox crossed the ride, but he would not have alarmed them. He did start a train of thought with me though. At this rather slack time in the fallow year, I could take some time off to watch foxes.

Furzy Common lay on the other side of Goose Lake, a high plateau of sandy heath with outcrops of rock and bracken, windy and bare on the summit like a lost stretch of Dartmoor, fringed with woods to the south where larks sang all day and foxes stole out at twilight, though in May, with cubs to feed, they were hunting all hours. My spies said a pair had been seen frequently going in and out of a small fenced-off area, an old reservoir, so one evening, without George, I climbed the steep side of Furzy Common and settled down under a gorse bush with the wind in my face, looking down on the tangle of heather and briar which had grown up ungrazed inside the north fence. This was only two strands of wire, but had served to keep out at least ponies and cattle. By one of the posts a deep narrow path had been worn through the tall grass, surely so worn it must lead to a den somewhere in the overgrown reserve.

A distant thunder of hooves meant the pony club were on their way home: one by one larks dropped from the cooling air, fell silent: a late bee droned past; something cold was crawling down my back — quickly forgotten. Nothing will ever blunt that stab of excitement when an animal first appears. Down the grass tunnel, a shape materialized, resolved into a narrow head, then a dog fox trotted out and began to nose in a leisurely way along the fence line. Big as an Alsatian, he had a distinctive coat, brindled red, brown and black, the general effect being unusually dark. He found something small, probably a beetle, pounced with both paws together, gobbled it up, but the hunting here was obviously poor and he soon moved away. A good beginning though.

I waited for vixen and cubs to appear . . . and waited. If you stare at a hole long enough, it begins to move. A blanket of cloud was creeping up from the west, so darkness would fall early. Maybe the whole family was having a picturesque romp on the far side of the reservoir. I moved cautiously down its western side; no paths came out there. Along the south though, a similar deep track led inside. It would be too dark to see soon, so, with nothing to lose, I crawled under the fence and followed the trail, though it was not easy, laced across with bramble at thigh level, intersected by branches of thorn and gorse. A tangle of honeysuckle in first bloom laid a wonderful sweetness on the twilight. The path never crossed an open space or passed a den, it came out again on the other side. The dog fox had simply been passing through.

Walking down the steep, sandy path which led off Furzy Common, I glimpsed two small shapes that could have been cubs, on the slope, then almost back on the road, I rounded a gorse bush and surprised a fox, very close in the almost dark. It leapt straight up in the air, gave a sort of strangled scream and shot off up the hill. I could just register it was a smallish adult, probably a vixen, with a pronounced white tip to the tail.

The next evening I decided to try an old sandpit, facing south, long overgrown with scrub thorn, two-foot-high sycamores and bramble, pitted with rabbit holes and the disused tunnels of an old badger sett. Fine weather had left no mud for paw prints, but the undergrowth was netted with interesting tunnels. A noisy rustling broke out almost at once so that I froze. It was the usual joker-blackbird making maximum fuss over finding supper. Half an hour later, with larks spiralling down, a fox trotted into view, a vixen with a very light ruff of neck fur. She disappeared purposefully into a tunnel among nettles and elders. When she reappeared later, head on, carrying a dead baby rabbit I could see her face was grizzled almost white along the narrow muzzle (a sign of age). Though the round dark eyes still shone keen and bright, she was obviously a very old fox and had possibly come here to hunt for herself rather than to feed cubs. Before dark I explored the pit; there were holes everywhere, but probably all rabbit.

Coming out onto the grass, I surprised another fox, this time a thin, rangy animal, probably a last year's cub with dark fur down its front legs like long black gloves. Foxes in plenty about, then, but I wanted to find a den and be able to watch a whole family. Inexperienced as a fox-watcher, I had probably gone about it the wrong way; I decided to return earlier next time and walk all the way round the common and over the top to get a better general view of the fox population and where they were most likely to den.

Of course, it did not work out like that at all. Next day George and I climbed up on to the ridge and set out to walk its length. Not really high, but a landmark in this flat country, the summit of Furzy is a fine, exhilarating stretch of level turf with views west and north into the far blue of distant counties; swallows skimmed overhead, flying down to Goose Pool for a sip of water on the wing. Short grass beneath the pads always has an intoxicating effect on George and he raced ahead, chasing anything that moved – lark, butterfly or rabbit. As the sun began to sink, little bats flittered overhead and pale moths appeared among the dry heather tussocks. Reaching the far end, we terraced along the northern slope: but never a sign of fox till we came near the old reservoir, where there was Brindle-back nosing along the fence again with his back to us. When I sank down on the grass, George automatically settled beside me, glanced at the fox, yawned, and looked pointedly the other way. (It had been a decent walk till now.) Brindle sauntered around, catching beetles, till disturbed by half a dozen Friesian bullocks on their way back to the farm below, as was their habit each night. By the time they had trundled soberly past, Brindle had vanished.

We skirted right round the reservoir without glimpsing Whiteneck or Blackgloves, but, rounding its lower corner, saw Brindle again, running uphill. Here one must report a sad falling off. Seeing something dog-size running away was too much for George. All training forgotten, he set off in gleeful pursuit, short legs a blur of speed and soon both had disappeared behind the gorse. Somewhere close by a rabbit thumped a warning in its burrow and gnats were dancing in clouds. I moved slowly on after the fox. In two minutes, George was back; his burst of speed is terrific, but shortlived. I said nothing, but he was so heavy with guilt, his legs gave out five yards away and he must crawl the rest on his stomach, eyes rolling with shame. I clipped on his lead and we continued on after the fox.

This brought us near the edge of the wood which 'slopes diagonally down to Goose Pool. I stood a moment, looking round for Brindle. The sun had set now, greens blurring to grey, patches of bedstraw showing up pale in the grass, the air cooling on the skin. Looking up the bank that borders the wood, I became aware of two fox cubs composedly watching me!

There was no cover. I sat down as slowly and steadily as possible. Even then one cub took fright and bolted down a hole in the bank; the other never moved. He was enchanting, puppy size with tall pointed ears, tipped with black, that seemed over-large for his alert little face. In fact he was not watching me at all, but George. As the air was so still, no dog scent had reached him; George could have been a short, dark cub, albeit with deformed ears! He watched us for five minutes, never moving, then ventured forward a few steps. Something small in the grass distracted his attention and he pounced, front paws together just like an adult, but it got away, so he went back into the hole. We had found a den at last, or rather George had. All was forgiven.

The hole was cunningly chosen, under overhanging fronds of bracken so that I did not realize at first that the cub had only gone just inside the mouth of it, was peeping out still. Then he jumped clear, stared at George with his feet spread and made a little whickering noise in his throat: come and play. While this fortunately had no effect on George, it brought his two siblings jostling out of the den, to fall upon each other in mock battle, each

trying to get his jaws round the others' neck, snarling, batting with paws, falling over each other, rolling down the bank, squeaking with excitement, sometimes breaking off to snap at flies or pant, tongues lolling, grinning open mouthed. They looked very well fed, showing podgy white tums when they fell rolypoly down the bank. Their faces were still blunt and roundish, but full of foxy spirit, wild and sly as they tumbled each other with little squeals and growls.

I watched them until dark, so we must needs walk home by starlight. Halfway down the slope, a fox barked, high and eerie.

Returning a few nights later, I went first to Goose Lake while the evening light was still clear. East of the rookery, along the far shore there had been a thriving heronry until the Great Storm had left their particular pine trees either flat on the ground or holding each other up at crazy angles. This spring I had only been able to locate three nests west of the rookery. Now I could see two tall heron fledglings teetering on the edge of a high nest; the whole business of herons nesting seems so awkward, with all those long legs having to be accommodated in a tree, wouldn't they be better on the ground like the waders? An adult flew in with a large fish crosswise in its beak and a tug of war ensued that threatened to unbalance all three.

Then my attention was distracted by surface matters, for sailing silently round the corner in mid-pool came the great crested grebes. The male dived, coming up close to his mate. He started to splash her with his beak, then tried head bobbing, comically up-down, up-down, all of which seemed to leave her unmoved, so he dived again, but she did not join in and I could soon see why, catching her in profile against the silvery water – a very small head and little straight beak stuck out from between her folded wings: the nestlings were having a ride. I watched her a long time, hoping she would swim nearer to the bank so that I could see how many chicks there were tucked away, but she stayed stubbornly in mid-lake, undisturbed by passing geese and mallard as silver turned to grey and long shadows netted the banks.

All at once a loud clamour of outraged squawks rose up from the opposite shore: herons were flapping up from another half dozen, unsuspected nests till the sky above the pines was filled with circling, protesting birds. The object of it all was a single buzzard threatening their nests from above on its blunt wings; surely a very hungry bird to consider attacking such large nestlings. They drove it higher and higher till it was forced to sheer off eastward, causing pandemonium in the rookery and a surge of cawing attackers to rise up from their nests and pursue it still further into the darkening sky. The herons flapped around in slow dignified circles for some time before finally settling back onto their nests. The buzzard had revealed there were at least nine nests in the pines, so the colony was slowly building up its numbers again.

Bats appeared over the lake and the first stars shone as the rooks at last returned to their nests, full of nestlings as big as themselves. It was too dark now to walk right up to Furzy Common and watch the foxes, only time to take George for a quick run up through the woods. A sunken sandy path led up to the wood's edge, its damp sides hung with hart's tongue fern and trails of ivy that half hid dozens of little burrows and tunnels. George tore about in the twilight chasing every faintest rustle of bankvole or woodmouse. A wren, woken from her roost, scolded us with loud 'tic-tic-tics'. The air smelled bitter and earthy from scuffed-up old leaves. By the time we reached the summit it was almost dark and there reeled out from just beyond the tree line that strangest of sounds, the harsh churring of a nightjar, thrilling in a spooky way, for the bird is getting rare in these parts.

Just as we turned back, there came another sound, one never heard before, a high wailing 'wa-wa-waa', quite close. Nothing had seemed to move, only a branch creaked overhead in a small night wind. The crying stopped, then broke out again, piteous and lost, 'wa-wa-waa . . .' George had crept up very close behind me. I realized we were right below the edge of the wood under Furzy Common where the foxes had their den. Was it a fox – a cub – caught in a trap? I would have to run all the way back to the car, get the torch, the dog rug to throw over its head, and were there some gloves? I stood frozen, knowing this would take a long time, but in the dark there seemed no other way of locating the sound. Could George find it? Above, the sky was still lighter than the boughs that interlaced across it: down here it was almost pitch dark.

When the cry came again it was louder, 'wa-wa-waa', then very loud as if the creature had turned right towards me, then it grew fainter and fainter as if running away though there was not the smallest rustle. At least I knew that it could move, so was not caught in a trap after all. I waited a long time, but heard nothing more, only the distant churring of the nightjar.

Soberly we made our way home, George keeping peculiarly close to heel.

Next evening it seemed imperative to go and see if the foxes were all right, though a wet grey mist cloaked the woods. Only a fox or possibly a badger could have made so loud a noise at ground level surely? The lane is miles from any house, so dog or cat could be discounted. Had it been trapped but managed to escape? Trapping was illegal in the forest. In any case there were no farm lands for miles where fox predation might have angered a farmer; it was all a mystery.

Under a dull sky, dusk was falling early as we walked over the brow of Furzy Common and down towards the bank, rabbits bolting away on all sides. Crouching down under a gorse bush and counting fence posts, I could locate the hole under its bracken curtain. At nine o'clock the vixen came out, sat up very tall on a hump of grass and did an in-depth survey of her front lawn. When at last she turned to go back, it was obvious she was White Tail, the one I had surprised in the old sandpit. After a minute she returned with two cubs. One mooched off, hunting small things in the grass, the other stayed still while the vixen gave first its ears, then its hind-parts, a thorough wash over. Watching the scene for a long time, I realized that the posts upheld small mesh wire netting to protect new plantings in the wood. Had a cub somehow got the wrong side of it and been unable to find the way back?

Though I stayed till dark that night and came many more evenings to watch the foxes, the third cub did not reappear. I shall never forget that piteous crying in the night.

On one of these visits, under a sky grumbling with thunder, I was walking down the slope of Furzy Common when a flick of tail betrayed a small group of fallow deer among the gorse below. There had been no activity at the den; the two remaining cubs were big enough to go off hunting on their own now.

No view of far counties either: a menacing grey pall shut out the world, dulled all colours to dun browns and growled threateningly, but in a clearing on the hillside, six heavily pregnant does were dancing – nothing skittish or undignified, just a stately pavane together with now and then a waltz turn, like the more portly members of an over-sixties club essaying a quadrille. As they gently cavorted, I could count nine fallow in fact, their summer white dapples bright and beautiful in the gloomy light. Young ones often play in the evenings, but I had never seen adults alone behave in this way. When a lone pony and rider came galloping full tilt along the track below, anxious to reach home before the storm broke, the dance broke up in some confusion, most of the deer running off downhill, but two pranced up towards me, revealed as handsome young bucks, their half-grown antlers in pale velvet. So they were the reason for the mothers-to-be excitement! Sexual behaviour among fallow seems to go on outside of the official season of the rut.

I would have liked to wait to see if bucks and does came back together, but the summit of Furzy is an exposed place at any time. When a jag of lightning split the sky, leaving the world darker, it was time to seek cover. Too late in fact, for halfway down the sunken path through the wood, rain began to fall, at first in isolated dollops, then in a steady downpour that hissed through the thick canopy. Moses, my father always maintained, controlled the weather. Before I reached Goose Lake, Moses had turned the tap off, though fat drops still drained from the leaves and fell splat on the forest floor.

As the storm rumbled away eastward, grey clouds parted in the west to reveal a long V shape of livid yellow light, like a shining creek between dark shores, and this was reflected far out in the still lake, the sudden brilliance drawing the eye so that at first I did not notice what was happening to the bank. It was moving.

Seething. Mare's-tails, comfrey and grass were still covered by a sheeny film of water and over them moved hundreds of little frogs and toads, offspring of all those hours of mating, each one no bigger than your fingernail, clambering and hopping through the jungle of stems, intent on a new life on the land. Fortunately the herons overhead were settled for the night.

Next evening, blue and warm, moorhens trilling across the lake, herons flying off to fish, a clamour of geese up the western reach, not a single frog or toad was to be seen, till I carefully rolled aside a half-rotten log. In a damp hollow beneath, three pairs of tiny black, gold rimmed eyes peered indignantly upwards. Gently I replaced their ceiling, even as a squawk high above heralded a heron's return to the nest.

Frogs and toads, herons and foxes were all successfully reared, but this was the first day of June, the month set aside for fallow maternity: any time from now on they could be dropping their fawns and it was my life's ambition to see one born and follow its first steps. With so many fallow about this may sound easy, but the herds break up, does go off on their own, becoming more elusive than ever and one could not go crashing through the shoulder-high bracken, for no deer must be disturbed in the quest. It was a real challenge.

The previous year a friend had told me where he had sometimes found new-born fawns hidden in a ferny ditch below the enclosure bank of an isolated wood sloping down from the heathy summit of Buzzard Hill, so on a warm June morning, George and I had set out. Fallow does hide their fawns away in cover, usually bracken, and leave them for quite long periods while they go off to graze. The fawns keep utterly still, camouflage being their only defence at this time and reputedly show no signs of fear at the approach of man, never having seen one before, so it seemed to me that George could be an invaluable help in scenting a fawn though he would certainly not lay a paw on it.

The way led up a long, long, deadly straight gravel track, between plantations of Scots pine, growing steeper as the day grew hotter. The warm air drew a lovely fragrance from the pines, an occasional large white butterfly or wood brown would fly up from tormentil and self-heal growing along the verge, but on the whole it was as uninteresting a track as you could find; even George looked bored, padding along, tongue lolling in the heat. A network of steep-sided drainage ditches made it impossible to get off into the aromatic shade of the trees. As we trudged on, buzzed by innumerable flies, I tried to conjure the picture of a tiny, dappled fawn lying alone in cool green ferns.

The noonday sun struck full down upon the gravel, but there was the gate ahead, leading out onto the heath. Leading in fact to a scene of desolation. The whole of Buzzard Hill had been burned. A few hardy tufts of grass stuck up here and there, otherwise the ground was black beneath gaunt black skeletons of burned gorse and heather.

Though the forestry workers would not have burned out ditches close to a wood edge, where we hoped to find the deer, it seemed unlikely that any doe would choose to give birth up here where there was nothing to eat. Not a bird sang: it was all as arid as the moon.

'That's no good then,' I said to George. 'May as well go home.' But he was already a black dot far down the track.

I decided to try the Island this year. Timing is difficult, since the very earliest fawns can arrive at the end of May, and the latest in July. The peak period is reckoned to be mid-June, but it seemed essential to start looking earlier than that to allow for trial and error, so we set out on June 7th, a warm, breezy morning, for the Island, a name only to be found in my head. It is really a small hill covered with bracken, heather and a scatter of birch and pine entirely surrounded by a sea of bog – not the quaking, horse-swallowing kind met with in *Lorna Doone*, but a vast slosh of peaty mud strewn with shallow pools after rain, but some of it firm enough to allow tussock grass to grow and to support small hooves. Isolation makes the hill a fascinating little world. Fallow often wander across to it, though few people find the narrow causeway which leads across the bog. To a mere human, the Island seemed an ideal maternity ward for fallow doe.

The causeway crosses one of the wettest stretches of the bog, where pools lie all year round. Here the pale, silky flags of cotton grass waved in the breeze, almond shaped, broad leaved pond weed float on the water, while the ground between was red with the deadly little leaves of sundew. A long-rotten log was totally covered in tiny plants, each round disc of leaf covered with bright crimson hairs and glittering pinheads of moisture lethal to passing insects. Turquoise damsel flies zigzagged over the pools, with one fat golden dragonfly; the mud of the causeway itself was patterned with recent hoofprints, leading ahead.

George was leashed up as we reached the Island itself; by contrast it was so dry and sandy the tracks at once disappeared. We sat down for a while to watch a crossroad of grassy rides, but only a green woodpecker looped across to his favourite dead pine and chaffinches sang their monotonous little songs, so presently we set out to explore one of the rides thoroughly. Bracken grew shoulder high, with dozens of little side paths threading through, just deer – or dachshund wide. We searched quietly through every one, finding here and there hoofprints, fresh droppings and small trodden nests under the fern where someone had lain. The bracken gave off a pungent, sour green smell in this altogether green world. A blur of tawny brown raised a flash of hope. I stalked carefully up a foot-wide path, round a bend – to find a neat, round patch of dead bracken. In fact we stalked several of these. At this point, George's report would have to read 'lacks interest'. He mooched along occasionally giving me a questioning look as to this lead business – who was there to harm? I should have taken more notice.

At the end of the ride we crossed over and began to work along the other side, watched by a pair of goldfinches from the nearest pine. 'Tuee tuee tuee,' they sang to each other, the sun showing up their red caps. Why had the does made this maze of paths if not to give birth? Did they come here to sleep? Had they borne their fawns and already moved on? And if so where? I was becoming expert at small ground flora, stitchwort and bedstraw, pale lemon cow-wheat, rusty sheep's sorrel. Midday now, drowsily warm, a woodpigeon 'croo-crooing' overhead – then, in the distance, that unmistakeable flick of fallow tail and the day was transformed.

If she had a fawn, all I had to do was watch her until she moved off to feed it, then follow. George now became something of a liability. We flitted closer till it was possible to see a fallow's latter half, now lying down, the front half hidden by a tall stand of bracken. Impossible to tell from that position whether she were pregnant or not, though there seemed to be something slightly protruding beneath the white rump patch, perhaps udders swollen with milk, or just possibly the water sac which breaks just before birth. Now and then a back leg kicked convulsively. Had I actually stumbled upon a doe at the moment of birth? George lay down and went to sleep in a patch of shade, but I was totally absorbed, prepared to stand for hours leaning there against a pine.

After a while it struck me that there should be more activity: didn't does usually stand up and move restlessly about while giving birth? It was frustrating not being able to see the whole animal, so in the end I did grow impatient, dropped on all fours and edged along till I could peer round the fern. Now only the front half of the deer was visible, but this did not matter anymore . . . It was a buck.

Drowsing away the noontide warmth, occasionally kicking out at flies, he was a handsome specimen with his half-grown antlers in pale velvet. He hardly glanced up when I laughed aloud, albeit with a trace of bitterness for those lost hours. Bucks are supposed to spend the summer in all-male herds.

We wandered all round the sandy knoll, scolded by jays who nest there; we found a fox earth cunningly hidden under a fallen holly, and the earliest pink sprigs of cross-leaved heath, but no other deer; all those footprints and droppings must have belonged to the buck, solitary king of the Island.

So I decided to return to the Castle and see what had happened to the several groups of deer which had frequented its ancient ramparts. Up through the wood, there was worrying evidence that forestry work had been going on – deep wheel tracks and piles of wood chips. All the deer might have fled. But what the forestry workers had done filled me with delight. Just outside 'the walls' by the high north-east corner, they had erected a culling platform, or high seat, reached by climbing a rough ladder of twelve wooden rungs. (Never mind that one of these was inscribed Not for Public Use.) From the top you could see practically all the land inside the Castle together with the track running past it, with a glimpse down the opposite ride; and deer seldom glance upward. It was ideal for doe watching, and still not yet mid-June. George, though, was not pleased. He stood at the foot of the ladder barking wildly, under the impression that I had turned into a squirrel, so it was no use looking for deer that day, though there were plenty of fresh droppings and acres of inviting bracken cover.

I came back alone, very early, with a cushion, food and flask, the great beeches still mere black silhouettes against the greying east. Just as I reached the Castle entrance a blackbird sang out high above and at once light and colour began to steal over the land, greening high branches and ferny floor. The sky faded to palest lemon, streaked with apple green, rabbits played among the bracken that shone with dew and a white barn owl flapped slowly homeward across a sky now turning flamingo pink. It was fresh and vernal as any Eden.

Before entering the Castle, something made me glance up the ride that climbs on eastward – and there on the crest, still and heraldic as some mythical beast, stood the white doe, silhouetted against the brilliant dawn sky, hazed about with golden light, marvellous as a unicorn.

I climbed the ladder and settled down, smug in the knowledge that much of the world still slept. Below, the rabbits came out again beneath the bank, the first bee scouts of the day zoomed over to a grove of foxgloves, a squirrel scampered along the bough of an oak in heavy summer leaf. From ground level the bracken would totally obscure what was going on, but from my perch I looked down into every secret path and clearing. All were empty, gilded with soft peach light till a menil doe trotted through the entrance and came at once to graze beside the ladder, followed soon by her yearling, presumably the one I had seen before, a little paler than his mother, the coat appearing to be white, splodged with pale coffee, his forehead sprouting six-inch antlers covered with velvet. He went off to graze under some birches at the far end. Was there any special reason why he had stayed with his mother, when most males wander off on their own in the spring? Would it make any difference if she were not pregnant? From above one could not tell.

As the sky shaded to the ordinary blue of fine summer, all the little forest birds had woken and tuned up, while the blackbird never ceased his whistling. By normal breakfast time the yearling had moved out of sight, but a common coloured doe came ambling through the gap, stood gazing round with big black eyes, then walked over to graze beside the menil, her coat a rich shining chestnut, in striking contrast with the lighter doe, in fact they showed each other off beautifully. But unless they had fawns already, such closeness was not a good sign. Does about to give birth are supposed to go off on their own.

As the sun climbed up the eastern sky, the Castle was netted with shadows: blackbird fell silent at last; midges came out and the white doe with her sandy yearling came running in, skidded to a halt and looked wildly round as if late for an appointment, then settled to grazing under the oak. Soon the menil ambled over to some trampled bracken and sank down to chew the cud, joined presently by common coat and lastly the white. Presently the younger ones pottered over and joined the family party. What luck to have the three distinct colours in one group: perhaps the only luck. Five hours since dawn and none of them had showed any signs of moving off to feed a fawn. From above all three looked fairly portly.

In all that time not one of them had glanced upward. By now I badly wanted a stretch and also to inspect them at ground level: a loose vulva and dropped udder are the signs of imminent birth. In the drowsy warmth of noon I inched down the ladder, but they saw me, were on their feet and bounding away in an instant. I let them go, out across the track, then followed; already they were grazing again along the green ride opposite, which suited my purpose very well. Skirting round through the wood I came up level with them but under cover of the trees. Well might a green woodpecker laugh in passing – the sight of a human trying to glimpse a doe's private parts must be truly comic. I was lying prone and trying to peer upwards through binoculars. Udders were a dead loss: all does, pregnant or no, keep their back legs close together in a most maidenly way.

So I gave up, stretched my legs with a walk round the pine plantation. Even these dull old trees bore pale green candles of new growth, as much as a foot on the tallest. Long shady brown aisles stretched ahead, just flecked with sunlight here and there, where it could finger down through the dense dark green canopy, then a sudden splash of bright yellow in the distance, big and bold. I wished George were with me. Small he may be, but would never let anyone creep up on me unawares or even lurk about near by. Still, a canary jersey seemed odd garb for any one who wanted to lurk in a dark wood. For a minute I stalked the blob of colour, flitting from bole to bole – and burst out laughing again. There, all alone in its private glade, blushing unseen like Thomas Gray's flower, stood a rhododendron bush thickly covered with bright yellow clusters of bloom and scenting the air all around with its indescribable fragrance, a blend of gorse and roses and something unique of its own: a garden escape far from any garden. I must be the only woman in Britain to have been frightened by a *Rhododendron luteum*.

When I returned to the Castle there were no deer in sight. Climbing back to the platform, I decided nevertheless to stay here and make it my headquarters for the rest of June. There was no future in running about after deer. As the afternoon wore on, only insects disturbed the silence, a rangy young squirrel ran up the nearest oak and out along the bough nearest to my hide. It sat up on its skinny haunches, turned its head to groom the small of its back, then, switching to the other side, caught sight of me, a human, incredibly at its own level! It sat bolt upright, wrung its paws together, chattered with fury and shot away swinging invisibly through several trees, though I could mark its passage by the shaking twigs.

Towards evening, as I had hoped, the does came back to the Castle, pottering at intervals through the gap, the same five spreading out to graze in the small clearings between tall stands of bracken. The menil doe seemed the tubbiest as she moved through her green world. When a pony and rider trotted down the gravel track, they all ran bunching together in the farthest corner, but soon relaxed again, their only movement the constantly flicking ears and tails as the evening gnats appeared.

So I came the next day, and the next. Once the menil yearling was missing for twelve hours, but rejoined them in the evening. On the second day another common coated doe joined them, but she had gone next morning. The five seemed to constitute a small permanent group.

Hour after hour I watched from my eyrie, sometimes discovered by a startled jay or magpie, but never by the fallow, chewed by midges, cramped and wonderfully content in my new role as honorary bird. One of them must be pregnant! On the fourth day the herd was still together till noon, when the menil doe and her yearling wandered off out of the south-west corner, the common doe grazed her way out of the entrance to move slowly along the verge, while the white doe and her yearling moved across it into the opposite woods. Something like this happened every day; towards evening they would all drift back as if the Castle's low banks gave them some added sense of security.

However, today the menil doe came back much earlier than usual, ambled about, grazing mouthfuls here and there in a restless sort of way, then stood close beneath me, staring through the trees. I thought she was listening for other deer, but none came. She had a half-hearted nibble, stared off in another direction, swung her head round to lick her left flank, ran a few yards, came to an abrupt stop and stared fixedly at a birch tree. Just as I was daring to hope this was the climax of all my waiting, she pottered nonchalantly off to the far end and began to graze again. But the next time she had a session of staring into space, she was broadside on, so I could see her straining, muscles tensed, black eyes very prominent, and she frequently peered round at her hind end as if wondering what was going on there.

About half past four she walked into some tall fern, turned round several times to trample it and lay down, only to get up again almost at once; she did this several more times, then stood still, straining, facing me but completely unaware. Something slithered down into the fern behind her; she turned her head quickly, lowering it to a pale blur amongst all the green, and a fawn was born.

Five o'clock. Her head moved rhythmically to and fro as she licked and licked while I longed for a better view. After a time she seemed to be nudging the baby, but it did not move, so there was another strong licking session, then more nudging as if she were trying to lift the small body from underneath. This time, the fawn, with a first huge effort, tried to stand, falling back at once into the bracken. Mother licked its ears in an encouraging sort of way. After a pause, it tried to scramble upright again, shaking all over, but managed to stay upright for a few seconds. The third time it not only stood, but staggered its first few steps in this new green world, coming into full view. So pale that it seemed almost white in the sun, and all fragile legs, it tottered against the doe, butted her flank and tried to suck her fur, but quickly decided this was a mistake, nosed about, at last found the udder, butted it with its little blunt forehead and began to suck, back legs wobbling wildly under the effort of keeping upright, mother meanwhile licking her hindparts.

Dappled mother and little staggering new-born among the sun flecked bracken made a picture I shall never forget; even the blackbird was moved to start singing again.

Some far away noise or drift of alien scent suddenly disturbed the doe. She lifted her head, neck tall, staring away from me, then turned back and paced slowly across the grass, baby desperately trying to keep up, tottering along, head level with udder so that I could glimpse a tiny male tassel, till she turned and headed him into a new patch of fern where he sank down out of sight.

She walked away ten steps, looked back, walked twelve and looked back again. Apparently satisfied that all was well, she turned her attention to herself, trying to lick her hindparts where the vulva hung loose and red. A few more steps, then she stood still to give the inside of her left leg a thorough grooming. After walking out onto the track, she paused to do the other hind leg. When that was finished she ambled across and a few yards up the grass ride where the rest of the herd were already having their evening graze. Once feeding herself, she seemed to forget all about her fawn, not so much as glancing back to the Castle till half an hour had passed, though she frequently swung her head round to lick her hindparts and udder. Grazing steadily northward, she and the small herd were soon lost to sight round a bend and my chance had come.

All my deer-watching life I had longed to have a close encounter with a new-born fawn. Climbing down stiffly from my seat I moved very slowly and quietly towards its hiding place. Well-meaning but ignorant people have been known to gather up the little waif of a new fawn and take it home under the impression it has been deserted. I looked along the opposite ride but there was no sign of mother returning, so I parted the fern and looked wonderingly down.

So thin! Just bones tautly covered with pale sandy and white skin. He was lightly curled round, blunt puppy-muzzle on hind legs, fur still wispy and damp, tall ears, long eyelashes, dark eyes wide open but not focusing to look at me. Because he was a menil, he had a wet muzzle the colour of milky coffee, and tiny pointed hooves to match. Hazy evening sunshine had as usual brought out the midges and they crawled all over him. In the end it was a moment of great concern, rather than delight. He looked so vulnerable and fragile – shouldn't his mother be hurrying back to give tender loving care? Hastening away I felt less and less scornful of ignorant townees as the evening wore on, repressing a strong desire to cover the little thing with a blanket and administer hot drinks!

The actual place of birth was just a trodden patch of fern with not a speck of blood remaining: evidently the doe had eaten the afterbirth and licked up all other traces so that nothing was left to alert the nose of a passing fox, the only enemy apart from well-meaning humans. When I returned to the high seat, mother had been absent for over an hour. There was no sign of the herd. A cuckoo flew over calling 'cock-cock,' something like a pheasant now that his voice had broken, and pale moths took wing below. As the sun fell behind the western woods a damp chill began to rise from the ground and still there was no sign of the mother doe returning.

Two hours now since the fawn was fed. Had she deserted it? Had she all along sensed that I was watching and so decided to abandon that frail little creature? I climbed down, slunk out of sight, walked about not noticing where, remembering those big dark trusting eyes. I did not return for half an hour, circling round to come into the Castle from the east. Peering round an oak, I could see nothing moving within the walls, so crept back and up to the platform.

From there I could see that the small herd, all five of them, had returned up the ride and were now grazing along the verge of the main track. A sneaking night wind rustled the light birch boughs together.

After another quarter of an hour, the menil doe lifted her head as if remembering something, trotted down the track, in through the gap, and stopped. Almost directly below me, ten yards from the fawn, she lowered her head and began to feed again . . . Nearly two and a half hours the baby had been alone in a new world with the grass growing cold and clammy . . . Oh come on, stop stuffing yourself – I had to resist the impulse to speak aloud!

At last madam paused, but merely because the common doe had trotted into the Castle. Has she come to give birth too? No, apparently just paying her respects, for both does move over to the bracken nest. At once baby staggers to his feet and takes three steps to meet them. Mother licks his ears. Aunt smells him over, and at last the fawn begins to suck, though only for a short time, because his legs fold up under him. Mother and aunt move a few yards away, grazing yet once more, but the fawn is gaining strength all the time now, struggles gamely up again, gangles over to mother, butts her udder and has another drink, then makes a little unsteady run away from her, lowers his head to sniff at a tree root, then totters back to mum. He makes several thirty-second forays into this huge new world, then stands still, wobbling violently. Like a foal, his stick legs seem far too long for the small body. Mother and aunt merely watched before. Now mother goes across to the tired fawn and noses him down into a new bracken nest for the night.

Next day, anxious to check on the fawn's progress, I set out for the Castle again, but, on the way, am drawn to look at a solitary goose by the lake. The narrow shingly beach is fringed with purple musk thistle just coming out, and the first sprigs of gold ragwort; the pool reflects blue sky patterned with broken white cloud like ice floes, round a hugh raft of white water lilies. Out on the water the crested grebes are diving, hardly breaking the reflections and far up the western reach rises a clamour of goose cries. But on the edge stands the solitary Canada, apparently guarded by a pair of ducks, sleeping on either side. Soon the dark brown female wakes, stands in front of him and flaps her wings, quacking loudly as if to say, 'Make some effort,' but the goose never moves.

Out on the lake a great flock of Canada geese comes gliding into sight round the willow bend, making purposefully for the shore, splendid big birds with black necks, white cheek patches and beautiful feather patterns, like quilting, on their brown backs. They wade ashore, stand all round the solitary one, though none actually touches him, and begin a vigorous preening session. This does rouse him at least to preen. It is noticeable now that his breast feathers look dirty compared with those of the rest of the flock. Suddenly a chestnut mare and her foal trot across the road and down the shore intent on a drink, scattering all the geese into the water. Two of the flock are the smaller, elegant barnacles, all black and white, probably a pair just passing through. Solitary now spends a lot of time drinking and it becomes obvious that there is something wrong with his neck – it is slightly crooked, and thicker than all the others. Soon he paddles back to shore, standing alone and forlorn as before, till the dark ducks swim over and settle down again on the beach, a foot away from him on either side.

A skinny little moorhen, half grown, still with gangly legs and a half-feathered look, arrives to peck about the shingle close by; the goose must loom over him. With a wild yelping out on the lake, the pair of barnacle geese smack the water with their webs, take off and circle northward, rising fast to clear the heronry pines. This upsets the Canadas who stand up and trumpet loudly, then sail back to shore, surrounding the solitary again. This time they settle down to sleep, heads turned to lie on backs. Solitary still stands staring stiffly ahead. Perhaps with that swollen neck he cannot eat properly? Of course a mere watcher should never intervene, but I cannot resist offering him a slice of bread.

Stupid not to have done this while he was alone: twenty-five large geese wake immediately and come crowding round as if starving, but solitary gets most of it, with a few crumbs for the

ducks who seem to be his self-appointed guardians. This is very odd behaviour in the avian world: most often a sick bird is set upon and driven away. The Canadas have gruff 'talking' voices for chatting to each other at close quarters. Disturbed by me, they come to a corporate decision, stroll off into the water and head out to the hidden reach, round the willow bend, leaving solitary alone again except for the faithful ducks who take up station again, one on either side. Then one of the receding flock looks back, and turns for the shore making soft 'prrp-prrp' sounds in its throat. Solitary seems to wake from some kind of trance, takes to the water, swims off and joins it, so they sail away together, just like the end of a sentimental movie! The ducks stand up, have a good stretch, flap their wings a bit, paddle out to the lily raft and begin to dive for food.

Goose Pool, full of mysteries, had detained me far too long. By now the ice floe clouds had drifted away: a hot summer afternoon lay on the land, so that it was a relief to dive into the shade of the woods. Not a leaf moved nor bird sang, only a deep hum of insects filled the still air as I climbed up to the Castle. The tall oaks and beeches were widespread enough for bracken to grow everywhere, green below green, all peaceful and lovely, but, from a practical point of view, splendid deer cover. As I softly approached the Castle, not a deer was to be seen, not so much as the flick of a fly-teased ear.

I climbed the platform hoping this might bring someone into sight, and, sure enough, far up the main ride, a whisking tail betrayed life. So the small herd was not far away, and the fawn hidden down there in the fern probably quite close to where he had been born. In places the bracken was my own height, though the fallow seemed to prefer three-foot stands, so I climbed down and began carefully to check round the banks, where the fern grew shorter, anxious to find but not disturb, treading softly, parting stems with care, buzzed by flies, trying to remember to check for adders underfoot, several times convinced of success, only to find a hollow full of dead leaves. After two hours and a complete circuit of the walls, I had found not a trace. The green woodpecker flew over, laughing in his jeering way, as well he might.

Up high, the cool evening air drifted with honeysuckle, I feared for my fawn. All skin and bone, so delicate and small, had it died in the night, been dragged away by some predator? A fox would kill a new-born fawn, for all there had been so little flesh on those spindly bones ... Surely the doe would not have taken its tottering little form outside the Castle banks? One could search the rides outside for ever. Obviously it was time to switch attention to mother and hope that she might lead me to the fawn.

The small herd was spread out, grazing through the woodland opposite; I could see the white doe quite close, moving in and out of the lengthening tree shadows, then a pair of riders came galloping full tilt down the main track, a piebald pony and a jet black, neck and neck. Long before the hoof beats had died away, the fallow had vanished. I climbed down and set off in search of them along the grass ride opposite as the evening moths flew out and midges danced in clouds above the ditches; I paused to peer into the bracken on either side, feeling hopeless now, guilty too. Rounding a bend I saw deer quite close and slipped into the eastern fringe of the wood to come upon them under cover.

I need hardly have bothered: they were intent on something else. The white doe and her sandy yearling, the menil and her pricket and the common doe were all standing round – the fawn – sometimes leaning forward to give him a lick, or a sniff, just like a doting group of aunts and uncles. The fawn's coat had darkened, was patched with warm coffee colour like his mother's and he was standing well, though slightly bent at the knees. I wanted to cheer!

Suddenly he arches his little back, kicks up his hind hooves and dashes off along the ride running like the wind, for a hundred yards at least. The yearling runs after him. Baby skids to a halt, butts the yearling's flank, even though his knobbly knees are wobbling a bit with all the effort. He runs back to the others, prances sideways into sandy yearling, then collapses into a leggy heap. Mother walks over and tries to nose him into bracken cover, but he jumps up and skips off down the ride again, wilful as a child.

Twenty-six hours since he was born: I would never have believed a fawn could make such progress in such a short time. Being a menil and in this unusual, small herd, there could be no mistake. So much for all those tales of fawns lying passive in the bracken day after day. Where had he spent his morning and afternoon? I should never know now. A blackbird was trying out his evening song as I took a last look, the sun fallen beyond the north-western trees. Fawn skips up onto a tree stump, jumps off, gambols round it three times, nips over to his mother and begins vigorously to suck.

ACORN COTTAGE

C LATTER-CLATTER! In the golden sunshine of late summer, the buck's coat shone golden bronze above his white underparts. Clatter-clatter, a noise like coat hangers knocking together as he swept his tall antlers across the low hanging branches of an apple tree at the end of the orchard, sending chips of bark and small twigs flying through the still, warm air. An apple fell, thump, and he paused for a moment, nosed about in the long grass, found it, crunched it up, then returned to his antler cleaning.

That velvet which had looked so beautiful on the Moon Hill fallow, having served its purpose in nourishing bone, was at last beginning to wither and itch, so it must come off. Clatter-clatter, as he swept across the branches again; long streamers of velvet were half scraped off, hung down over his face: it must all be stripped away and the antlers hardened before the huge excitements of the rut. Three peacock butterflies and a red admiral fed together on one spike of purple buddleia, the fragrant old garden was full of the drowsy hum of bees.

For all the stillness, the top bough of another orchard tree shook to and fro; a squirrel ran along it, grabbed an apple, then sat bolt upright to eat. The fruit was not nearly ripe yet, should stay on the tree till October. The squirrel ate the side that was flushed red, then threw the rest pettishly down onto the grass, before snatching another and treating it in the same way. Working at top speed, the squirrel leapt to a lower branch, whipped off another apple, black eyes shining, tail and flanks glinting gold in the sun, though down its left side stretched three parallel black stripes where the skin had been raked by sharp talons.

Attracted by the thud of more apples, the buck left off fraying and ambled up through the orchard, crunching up the rejects – six fell in as many minutes – wading deep in Michaelmas daisies, disturbing a cloud of little orange gatekeepers. He had particularly large white spots and tall antlers; though widely palmated, they were most elegant, but not quite individual enough for my purpose.

Acorn Cottage huddles deep in the forest, in a hollow where mist lies on autumn evenings, woods enclosing it on three sides with a stretch of open grass in the front bordered by birches and wild cherry. Squat and square, built of stone and thatch for a keeper, with a well for water and oil lamps for light, it has long been abandoned and is slowly being returned to the wild. The thatch has blown away, leaving a few rafters across the sky and a small

outhouse still roofed with corrugated iron. A five-foot birch waves from a chimney on the broken gable end. There a pair of wagtails raised a brood of seven chicks in the spring which still flit about the ruins, flicking tails, paler and greyer than their smart black-and-white parents.

This was to be my camping place for the autumn, from which to watch the fallow rut. I wanted to find a buck with some instantly recognizable feature, who could be followed week after week: a white one would be ideal but too much to hope for. The buck in the old, overgrown orchard crunched a last apple and trotted off into the eastern pines, strips of velvet floating out behind his antlers like hair ribbons. A blackbird was busy gobbling beakfuls of rose hips where a rambler had straggled all along the broken fence, but no birds sang in the sultry August warmth.

Though I had been coming to Acorn Cottage for a long time, the woods stretched for miles around it on every side and much of them was still unknown territory, so on September 1st I returned with George to go exploring. As we walked through a gap in the fence into that jungle of a garden, a robin sang out from the rambler rose, a piercing sweet sad song: autumn had come.

Fallow were on the move everywhere, in beechwoods and heathland, larch spinneys, lawns and dark pine plantations, small groups of does and their fawns, solitary bucks, once five together and once a black buck with majestic antlers who vanished away in the dim aisles of a fir wood and could not be found again. Sweet chestnut leaves began to turn yellow, misty mornings left every spider's web spangled with water drops, thistledown drifted over the old garden where orange chrysanthemums struggled to bloom in the forest of grass, and the cherry leaves flushed pink. Miles and miles we walked in this lovely, lonely part of the forest, seldom meeting anyone, for all the tracks were gated against cars. Undisturbed, the fallow evidently flourished here, but as yet I could find no individual to follow. Bucks were moving over long distances and too fast to track. Last year's rutting grounds lay under drifts of dead leaves, not easy to find.

October 1st: bracken turning amber along the rides, birches showing yellow leaves among the fountain fall of green, chestnuts thudding down. George and I had been out all day, turning back late afternoon as a wet mist began to fall, cutting visibility to just a few yards. We were walking along the bank of Blackley Water through an oak wood with an understorey of holly which kept off some of the rain. A blackbird sang out briefly, then fell silent, so there was only the babble of the stream where it met a fallen branch, a distant chainsaw and the splat of falling acorns. Late for forestry men to be working. George had raced off after a squirrel; when I caught up, he had a record – three squirrels up one tree! They peered down at him with switching tails spitting with anger, while he stood panting below, eyes shining with glee.

'Come on, you old fool!'

Then something clicked into place: it was not *George* who was the fool. In spite of the rain I turned round and set off back the way we had come. Of course foresters did not work this late; that was no chain saw – it was the distant sound of a mating call from a red stag.

As the call seemed to be coming from the east, we had to leave the path and set off across the forest floor through the reddening leaves and prickly tentacles of dewberries, over dead branches and hidden ditches with the light fading and the mist turning to rain, but nevertheless hot with excitement. At last we broke out of the wood on to a vast flat stretch of heath, sere and brown under the grey sky. All was silent. Then the roaring broke out again, quite close. Self-seeded pines straggled out onto the heath for several hundred yards and somewhere in their midst was a red stag.

Here the walking was, if anything, more difficult, through wiry old heather bushes thigh high. George's lead kept tangling in the stems, but he bounded gamely on. Every footfall must be tested since feet were invisible; once we did fall headlong into a hole; it was really slow going and the light fading fast. I leaned against an eight-foot pine to listen, and heard quite close, for the first time that season, the guttural mating cough of a fallow buck. Had I made a mistake then and it was a fallow all the time? No, from further away came the stag's bellow, and for a time I stood there wet through, facing a long dark walk home, but shaking with laughter at this extraordinary duet, as blaring bellow and belching cough sounded out alternately across the darkening heath. Were they oblivious of each other, or each trying to hold territory?

A rustle much nearer than buck or stag and three dark shapes materialize from the pines; there is just light enough to make out two red hinds and a young one. They run off, then stop and one of the hinds trots back to peer at me round a tree – maybe she can smell George but not see him, down in the heather, and is intrigued. As we blunder back to the nearest path, the buck has stopped belching, but the stag is still roaring out his challenge. He would probably stay on this territory, since hinds were already drawing in to him. I must come back in daylight! Reds always start their rut about a month before the fallow, for all the buck was starting to call.

As it was now pitch dark without even stars to light us home, we had to go a longer way round on gravel tracks. In half a mile, one of them brought us past a keeper's cottage, where the keeper himself was just calling his dogs in for the night. Had he seen the stag, I asked.

'Walks past my place every morning at half past seven sharp. Twelve pointer he is, real big'.

'So if I come down tomorrow morning . . .?'

'What time?'

'Half past nine.'

'Right. By then he'll be out beyond those pines, near where you heard him tonight. But if you wait a few days there'll be more hinds drawing in.'

'He won't vanish if I do wait?'

'No, no, be here another month, I reckon.' We said goodnight through the rain. As I turned for home, he called after me. 'I wouldn't exactly go shaking hands with that ol' stag if I were you . . .'

After all my fruitless wanderings, it was wonderful to have a guaranteed deer-watching place. A week later I came back, on a mild misty morning, the sun struggling to shine through a high golden haze, revealing what I had only glimpsed in the twilight, a long stretch of heath distantly ringed with woodland and roughly cut in halves by the river, hidden among oaks and holly. It was easy to splash across one of its shallower stretches heading west. Half-way over, a distant bellowing broke out in the east, so I stopped in midstream, yellow oak leaves eddying past my boots. When the bellow came again, it sounded more like the rounded moo of cattle, so I waded on, coming out into the open with the heath spreading away ahead and the keeper's cottage a white dot at the wood's edge on my left.

The tall old heather bushes still bore a few sprigs of purple flowers here and there. Ponies and cattle had trodden narrow paths through them which made walking much easier; soon I was halfway to the seedling pines, chaffinches flying up, a plump partridge bustling into cover, ambling ponies disturbing a magpie, but of deer no sign at all, not even through the glasses, only a sea of dull browns, dead bracken, dying heather, colourless grass. All quiet among the pines, only a flicker of white as three wheatears flitted away – and then that most unmusical of sounds, but Bach and Beethoven to me, a deep, grating roar, quite close; out on the heath a patch of bracken began to move!

It was like watching a fuzzy photograph come slowly into sharp focus. A whole herd of red deer had been there all the time, lying down chewing the cud in this north-west corner, a half moon of heath fringed by pine woods. Three hinds had stood up, while six or seven more heads showed above the heather. The nearest hind was a warm orange-brown with a darker neck and a pale rump shading from orange to white. After watching fallow so much, their sheer size always takes me by surprise, but just then the stag rose to his feet, making even the hinds look small, a magnificent great beast, less red than the females, with an orange behind, greyish face, dark neck and those huge spreading black antlers, their twelve points paling to bone colour. When he threw back his head and roared at the sky, it was a harsher, rougher sound than that of a bull. At the end of the roar he broke into short quick bursts: those were what sounded like a chain saw, at least in the distance.

In leisurely fashion the whole herd was coming to its feet, eight hinds and five calves, their coats lighter and browner than the adults. One ambled over to its mother, sucked briefly, then returned to grazing. The stag suddenly lowered his head and made for a hind, but she ran away, fast. He chased another; she ran, though only a little way. When she stopped, he smelled her rump with interest, then made to mount, but she walked away. They circled each other slowly till she got tired of it and sat down, which

111

made him raise his head and blare out his frustration over the heath; he even galloped off a short distance.

Soon he was back though, chasing another hind, and another, and another, but none of them would actually stand long enough for him to mate. In half an hour they were all sitting down again, so, with a final despairing roar, he settled down too. Eight wives and no satisfaction! Obviously none of the hinds was really on heat yet. There was no sign of any other males. Once lying down the herd blended almost invisibly into the heath, even a pale ear flicking off flies might have been a dead leaf blowing in the wind.

It was the third week in October when I returned, the river higher up the boots, swirling along a wonderful carpet of bright leaves. The oak leaning over the water was full of squirrels, one unaccountably running to and fro with a yellow holly leaf in its mouth; another was picking and eating acorns with what Jane Austen would call feverish haste, while a third was just playing. He was the smallest squirrel I have ever seen but already had a thick coat. He chased his bushy tail, dashed along a branch, swung down to the one below, almost fell off, remembered his tail and made a paw swipe at it, then whisked out of sight. On this grey morning, water-light danced over the oak boles and a grey wagtail pecked about the shallows, his yellow breast reflected in a still pool, but another shallow was a whirlpool of broken light, seething with hundreds of tiny silver fish. As I waded ashore a woodpigeon 'croo-crooed' overhead and missel-thrushes flew off from a bright-berried holly.

Compared with all the activity along the river, the heath looked lifeless and vast under an overcast sky: it was exactly nine thirty as I reached the young pines, and there they were, in the same place, only the resting herd seemed larger. Almost at once, His Majesty rose up and roared and the hinds began slowly to rouse themselves. The keeper had certainly been right about more hinds arriving, for there seemed to be at least fifteen of them, most with calves; the herd looked really big now they had all stood up. The stag ran after the nearest hind who sidled away, but let him catch up and mount her. As soon as his brief bliss was over, she turned and mounted him! This was just the first of the morning's surprises.

The hinds spread out to graze, many with fine, smoothly shining russet coats, others more brown, among the duller calves, their rumps comically bright, the only dabs of colour on this grey morning. Dead heather spread away, dun and dark to an horizon of black pines. On the western edge of the herd, another stag was grazing, a young one with only six-point antlers. He made no attempt to chase any of the hinds; he would probably wait his chance to the end of the rut, when the King might be too exhausted to care any more. Late-born calves, kids and fawns have to contend with a double handicap: not only have they less growing time before winter sets in, but they were probably sired by lesser stags or bucks.

After a lull, His Majesty throws back those splendid black antlers, utters a prolonged bellow and runs after a mouse-coloured hind who takes off straight for the seedling pines, which are splendid cover, but little real protection. Through the glasses the stag is as big as a bull and far too close! Fortunately his mind is on Mouse, who slows down, dances sideways and stops. When he catches up, she turns and rubs her face against his; though this looked a tender gesture, she probably had itchy insect bites, I thought sceptically, expecting the mating of these most bovine looking deer to be as quick and business-like as bull with cow. But I was wrong.

The stag smelled her over gently, then for a time she rested her head in the middle of his back, before moving round to rub faces again – he seemed to enjoy this, rubbing against her muzzle too, but he did not initiate any of these seemingly 'loving' gestures. Finally they did mate. Perhaps this was his favourite wife, with special privileges?

Some of these intimate moments could only be described as comic. A rather pale hind ambled through the herd, stationed herself just in front of the stag, lifted her tail accommodatingly and stood at the ready. He studied her backside consideringly for a while, then lay down! The hind's running away seems to be a necessary trigger, not just a female ploy.

The next courtship was another tender affair, though again it was the female making the running. A fine, deep rust-red, she ran away a few yards, stopped, waited, mounted the stag and proceeded to rub her chin all over his back. After another little run they stood head to tail while she rubbed the whole length of her flank against him breaking off only to gentle faces together and presently to mate.

While all this was going on, two more stags had appeared silently out of the woods. They came trotting eagerly up to the herd, then paused and fell to grazing on its eastern fringe, taking no apparent notice of the hinds. After each burst of activity, His Majesty tended to lie down for about ten minutes. He seemed not to have noticed the new arrivals. In any case, they were younger deer, their antlers mere twigs compared with those wicked twelve points.

About mid-morning, while the stag and his latest consort were caressing cheeks together, all the hinds slowly stood up, joining the calves who were mostly up and grazing already. The whole herd was a splendid sight, some thirty deer altogether and, at the heart of it, the great stag mounting his loving hind yet one more time, lifting his head for a last triumphant bellow. Then he turned his head to the north, away from me, and set off at a run for the pine woods, all the herd running too, even the young stags on its outskirts. Nothing had frightened them; this was obviously the next move of the day. In a moment the heath was empty, but for a late lark spiralling up from a clump of reddening whortleberry. Soon even the roaring had died away.

Just as I turned southward, the sun broke through, painting the mixed woods ahead copper and orange, russet and bronze, quilted with yellow and green. Once inside I trod a wonderful coloured leaf-carpet all along by the river, one bend of it choked with fallen crab apples shining scarlet in the water: a deer feast. Halfway to the bridge, a distant commotion made me slip behind a tree, peer ahead; soon half a dozen piglets careered out onto the path, jostling and squeaking, falling over, rolling about, little eyes shining, dashing to and fro, comic little grey beasts each with a neat pink belt. Eventually mother appeared, a large Wessex saddleback, her pink trimming more of a cummerbund. She was pottering sedately about under an oak, doing the job for which she had been sent out into the forest, gobbling up acorns. All told there were ten piglets, as yet too drunk with freedom to think of eating.

Outside Acorn Cottage, a horesbox was drawn up: half a dozen young Tamworths slithered down the ramp and rollicked off at once into the woods. With their long snouts and hairy ginger coats, they resembled the wild boar who had once roamed the forest. They would do well, for this autumn was especially rich in 'mellow fruitfulness'. Round the cottage wilderness, hawthorn branches were weighted down with crimson berries; the briar thicket normally beloved of tits had been taken over by thrushes greedy for the scarlet hips. All through the woods there were heavy crops of beechmast and sweet chestnut, as well as acorns, so unless there was an exceptionally hard winter, squirrels would be swinging from every twig come the spring.

Early morning in the wild garden, the air shining with dewy spider webs and floating thistledown. Long strands of gossamer trailed across the ramblers and a flock of bright goldfinches descended on a stand of teazles in the corner. The robin sang his first small song of the day from the nearest apple tree and from far in the woods sounded a deep gutteral coughing; the love song of a fallow buck.

All the red-deer watching had set back my plans for the fallow, so George and I set off at once to trace the sound and perhaps find a rutting stand. It was a fortunate chance to hear a buck calling at this hour since the fallow rut is an altogether more secretive affair than the red, taking place deep in the woods and mostly after dark. No sooner had we set off southward through the oaks, where the Tamworths were enthusiastically at work, than the calling stopped. Sometime later it broke out again, to the east – surely a different buck – so we turned off into an unknown part of the forest, all dark pine plantations. This was hopeful, since the fallow often choose conifer woods for their rutting floors (areas they trample to mud where mating will eventually take place). Under a sky of pale, cold blue, the pines hardly rustled; sound would travel well in such still air. This buck had now stopped. We stood listening at a crossroads, tall pines spreading away on every side. No sound at all but a distant drumming of hooves. Trying to visualize the map, I thought the right-hand track led out eventually on to heathland, so we took that since fallow bucks often seem to choose a stand near the edge of woods.

We turned the corner. Twenty feet away a handsome buck with

his back to us was busy fraying the lowest branches of a pine, tossing his antlers to and fro, sending twigs and needles flying. Close beside him were two does, who obviously had been watching in admiration, now staring at us. Surely they would break for cover any moment, alarm the buck and all vanish. I cursed myself silently for not having leashed George before, then stopped. He was some yards ahead on a squirrel scent, and the does had not moved: they were watching him, ears pricked, craning their long necks to see over the tall bracken along the verge. As soon as he was out of their sight, they trotted off through the fern after my little decoy, still peering inquisitively ahead at his small black person.

Meanwhile, I could watch the buck. Still in chestnut summer coat with big white dapples, and tall antlers not widely palmated, he could have been the buck who stole apples from Acorn Cottage orchard. He seemed intent on one tree, swinging vigorously to and fro, leaving the twig ends white and chewed. He did not seem to miss the does, or notice me; it was a lesson in concentration. Was this the buck I had heard calling? At last he slowed down, stopped, eyed the broken branches, sniffed at them and finally made off into the close-planted conifers.

Was his rutting ground in there? Not wanting to call out loud I had first to go on down the track to find George. Rounding a bend I came upon him trotting back and, just beyond, a gate out onto the heath. (The does had vanished.)

So we went through to explore along the southern boundary, but this was a mistake; we seemed to have walked into a Western. I grabbed George up as three riders swept very close past us, shouting, 'They've got six.'

'You take the east side.'

'Look out for Harry's grey.'

We had inadvertently joined a round-up, when the free wandering ponies are brought in to be checked, wormed and branded. Out on the wide expanse of heath to the west, the drumming of hooves grow louder and half a dozen ponies appeared bunched together, pursued by riders yelling, 'Coom on, coom on!' A small crowd in wellies and very old jackets was stringing out in a line to funnel the ponies into a rough wooden pen which stood against the enclosure fence with its gate open.

'Hey, you over there, lend us a hand.'

So I found myself part of the human fence, cheering as the ponies came thundering by, manes and tails streaming, and were jostled into the pens. Labradors barked; horseboxes backed up; the ponies milled about steaming, wild-eyed at this sudden confinement.

'Milly's got a foal!'

'Come on, there's three more over by Pinkham.'

The riders set off again, red-cheeked and eager; it was rather exciting, an air of carnival mingled with a strong smell of horse, another autumn rite taking place all over the forest, but not actually the one I was looking for.

During the next few days, I tried to follow a black buck, a buck with a misshapen left antler, any buck, realizing in the end there was no future in this. Fallow were certainly drawing in to the woods round Acorn Cottage, but they were also ranging far over the forest. Late one afternoon a buck began to call not far from the cottage. It is an extraordinary sound; it sounds almost painful, a cross between retching, belching and coughing very deeply. At once three does appeared in the orchard, heads up, ears high, listening raptly: obviously it was Mozart to them. After five minutes one of them must have said, 'Do let's,' and they trotted off down the track followed by their two fawns – and me.

A chill, grey day after two nights of rain, pines black against a dun sky, but strange new colours were appearing along the verges, under the trees purple russulas still holding rain in their concave caps, slimy brown paxillis by a clump of birch and further on more russulas, this time bright yellow. With the ground so soft, it was easy to follow the neat hoofprints where the does had swerved off the track into the pines. Even through the needle carpet the narrow, disturbed line was plain to see; probably they were following a path already trodden for them. Here at the foot of a rogue birch grove was the pixie toadstool, fly agaric, its pretty, white tufted, scarlet cap announcing its powerful effect.

The tracks disappeared where a pine had fallen, but reappeared on the other side. The buck was no longer calling but other does were flitting silently down through the trees on a path parallel with mine. The tracks emerged from the conifers onto a path between tall oaks and beeches, chestnut, ash and birch, flaming yellow, copper and orange, light and colour at last; the ground was still carpeted with bright leaves, clear yellow ash, tawny sweet chestnut, green and mustard oak. This path made a kind of terrace, but the hoofprints crossed it, and wound away down a long slope towards a further pine plantation. I settled down on a fallen beech with a good view across the sloping wood. Several does ran away when I came out of the pines, but they soon came back and fell to grazing here and there among the tall beeches. All seemed quiet, then came a flicker of movement high up in the dimness of the pines – antlers!

Squirrels whisked about everywhere, mostly harvesting sweet chestnuts; the burrs lay about, brown and prickly like families of small hedgehogs. A robin sang out from the nearest ash. By my seat grew clusters of deep purple-blue fungi, the amethyst deceiver and, on the trunk itself, the hard shell shapes of ganoderma, sprinkled with spores the colour of cocoa. Though I watch the wood all the time, I do not actually see him appear – suddenly, in typical fallow fashion, he is there, a splendid buck in his prime, with great palmated antlers curving round almost to meet each other at the tips. At once he lifts his head and lets forth a stomach-heaving, gutteral bellow. Against the dark pines his coat glows a deep gold, except for his neck, which is black from rolling in the mud.

He proceeds to stalk up and down, stiff-legged, proud, belching now and then, also lowering his antlers to churn up the mud. Is he actually laying out a new rutting ground? Does and fawns in twos and threes continue to graze placidly across the slope; in contrast with his elegance, they were already growing their brown winter coats, tending to look dull and scruffy: peculiar garb for courting time; roe are much better dressed for theirs.

With a last belch which sends his antlers almost scraping his back, the buck hurries away into the pines. Several does stop feeding, turn to watch him go with moss still hanging from their mouths and finally decide to follow, vanishing away into the gathering shadows.

Is there already a rutting stand deeper in the woods then? With the coming of dusk, belching breaks out far to the left and nearer, to the right. I resolve to come back and explore in daylight.

Another night's rain brought up brilliant scarlet russulas under the birches, and tiny yellow umbrellas on the verge. By the afternoon all the cloud had shredded away and a still, golden light lay on the land. Because there had not been a hard frost yet this autumn, the bracken had not shrivelled but turned palest shining gold, seeming to light the sloping wood from beneath.

This day I had come earlier to the beech seat, disturbing a cloud of little birds, chaffinches, great tits and a nuthatch. Three or four does spread about the wood with their fawns, glanced up, stared in an indignant way, then returned to grazing unconcerned. No sign of antler nor sound of belch as yet, so I decided to go down into the pines and look for the rutting floor. But what looked like an easy ferny slope from above proved to be impenetrable ground for a human; no wonder the deer move about so freely with no fear of intruders. The ground was threaded by an intricate maze of deep ditches half choked with old fallen branches, half of them rotten, and small rhododendron bushes, pitted with sudden watery holes and patches of gluey wet clay, the whole tastefully carpeted over with fallen leaves so that it was impossible to see where one's feet were going.

After floundering about making far too much noise, I managed to reach yesterday's parade ground, a mere eight-foot circle of bare earth trampled to peaty mud, but there was no mistaking the smell! To render themselves totally irresistible to the females, bucks blend their own brand of aftershave, then roll in it, which was obviously what the buck had been doing the previous day. It is a rich mixture of earth and urine, melded into mud for extra stickability.

Since the way forward into the pines was so treacherous, I retreated up the slope to my beech seat. In spite of my crashing around, there were more fallow grazing under the oaks and beeches, several does with fawns close to them, two prickets who kept together and, furthest away, a buck. Not the King, though: this one was smaller, with only narrowly palmated antlers. He seemed merely to be loitering, chest deep in tawny bracken, and quite silent.

Leaves fell from the flame-coloured beeches and tiny brown scales drifted through the stillness into my hair; high above a squirrel was feasting on beechmast and discarding the roughage. Far away, at the limit of hearing – was that a buck's call? Yes, it certainly was, for all the does lifted their heads and pricked their ears towards the pines; nothing happened, so they returned to feeding, but five minutes later another buck walked into view quite close, stood and stared about, then trotted over to the aftershave patch, snuffed at the ground, threw back his head and uttered a loud, throaty challenge. For all he was so close, the does never looked up.

He was a splendid buck in his prime with a sparsely dappled, dark gold-brown coat and wide antlers branching out almost straight on either side. He strode over to a six-foot sycamore, lowered his antlers and began to thrash it to pieces. Soon the seedling tree was reduced to a slim trunk with a few pale frayed stubs on the top, like brushes. Lifting his head at last, he saw the nearest doe and chased her, but she ran away more than the usual token distance, so he gave up, and wandered off, as the sun fell below the pines.

With the twilight, excitement creeps through the woods, does move together in groups, grazing forgotten. When a belching cough sounds out, very close, from just inside the pines, all heads turn that way – and there he is, King Buck with his great curved antlers and pale coat, standing motionless at the foot of the slope. The wood seems to hold its breath.

A squirrel breaks the spell; in no way awed by any old deer, it dashes across the forest floor and swings up into an oak, startling a blackbird into flying off 'pink-pinking' with alarm. Stiff-legged, King Buck walks up the slope to Dark Buck. Six feet away he stops and stares. Dark Buck walks slowly forward and jostles his shoulder. For a full minute they stand motionless, side by side, then set off parallel with the edge of the pines, walking with measured pace. The does watch them go. When they have passed my beech I follow, knowing what is going to happen.

Unhurried, they keep side by side till the wide track through the pines comes in sight and they swerve off towards it. Once on the gravel there is no way I can keep out of sight, but neither pauses to look back, moving a little faster now, then suddenly turning off, straight into the pines. Out of my view they must have paused for a sizing up, staring match again, for the first terrible crack of antler comes only as I draw level and can watch them in the narrow, shadowy arena of a conifer aisle.

They strain together, forehead to forehead, back legs braced at an angle, eyes bulging, neither giving an inch till they break apart, only to clash again with that heart-stopping sound like a dozen breaking bones. This time Dark Buck drives the King back a foot, only to be shoved back in his turn; to and fro they force each other, neither giving more than a few inches each time. Drawing away once more, each flings himself upon the other. Though the King has seemed the larger animal, it is really only his antlers, so widely palmated as to give him an advantage; enough this time for him to drive Dark Buck back a good six feet. This time, when they break away, both turn and head for the gravel track, their breath a mingled cloud on the chilled air.

Once on the path, they trotted briskly off the way they had come, through the dusk, still together. This seems to be the general pattern of buck fights, moving off side by side to find a secluded spot, even leaving it again the same way. It appears to an observer to be curiously lacking in emotion, a rite to be carried out rather like an arranged duel, pistols at dawn. When they reached the beech wood, Dark Buck swung off to the south, while the King returned to his stand and does began skittering about in the bracken, only their pale underparts and white rumps showing in the gathering dark. The young buck had all this time scarcely moved.

As I groped my way up the slope, the King let out a huge, prolonged belch of triumph: challenge me if you dare! From close by came a very small bleat-bleat. Even in the rutting season, it is seldom one hears a doe speak: when she does it is a very gentle, feminine sound.

By the time I reached Acorn Cottage, a hard, cold sky blazed with stars and a huge orange moon was rising over Vixen Wood to the east, just the night for the gooseberry jam. Several evenings lately, when about to go home, I had glimpsed a badger crossing the bottom corner of the orchard. Tonight I would wait and hope to see him properly, perhaps find his sett. Friends of mine had enticed neighbouring badgers into their garden by putting out bread and honey. Being of a frugal turn of mind, I had brought a stale loaf and a pot of gooseberry jam so mature that it emitted alcoholic fumes!

Starting in the orchard corner, I laid a trail of jammy bread through the long grass, right up to the cottage doorway. If no night animal relished it, all the resident little birds would soon clear it up come daybreak. I settled down on the broken sill of a glassless window. Crooked black tree shadows striped a silver orchard. A very small rustle, and a bank vole who lived under the walls was nipping neatly up one of the leaning fence posts. He seized a rose hip from the old rambler, and sat upright to eat it, a podgy little figure, bulging eyes shining in the moonlight, but halfway through dropped it, to shoot down the post into sheltering grass; stealthy small rustles came and went as the moon rose higher. Once a buck called, startlingly close, but moving away. Very cold, very still and nine o'clock: badger time. Suddenly 'whoo-oo-oooo' floated out over the forest from just above my head: the tawny owl was perched on the roof. Creeping along, I was just in time to see the male glide silently away like a pale moth.

Turning back I caught a movement halfway up the orchard: a dark shape, the moon gleaming on its white face stripes. A badger was moving slowly, purposefully up the jammy bread line straight towards me, so it seemed best not to move. Soon he was level with the cottage corner, bundling along, snuffling and gobbling quite loudly, a smallish animal, probably born this year, the tiny eyes in the black face stripes somehow giving him a vulnerable, don't hit me, look.

He followed the bread line to my feet, snuffed my boots loudly with his wet black snout, paused a moment to stare up shortsightedly into my face, then ambled across my insteps to gobble up the last piece of bread with lip-smacking enjoyment, the moon silvering his grey fur kilt and tab of tail. For a while he stayed, snuffling hopefully about, but finally realized this was the end of the trail and ambled off across the track into the darkness of the pines. Was he drunk that he came so close? Certainly not. I know now from further experience that he would come every night just for plain bread and providing I made no sudden movement would sit down to eat it by the cottage door in the full light of a torch.

Next day I investigated the orchard corner and there was a badger path plain to see, a smooth bare line worn down the side of a deep ditch and up the opposite slope into the conifers, continuing on as a shallow flattening of the needles a hundred yards through the trees, then swinging round to a half-felled area close beside the gravel track. A few trees had been cut down and many more brashed, their lower boughs left strewn about, so of course the path disappeared into a wilderness of spiky dead pine branches. I stared at this, disappointed not to find the sett after such a promising path, then, catching sight of some pale, raw-looking earth beneath the interlacing twigs, realized this was the sett. Exploring with difficulty across the strewn floor I found half a dozen old, half choked entrances, and three obviously in current use, soft new soil deeply printed with the wide badger paw. One had a mat of used bedding thrown outside, and, close by, a latrine pit, its contents full of iridescent beetle shards. Half hidden among the brash were new pine seedlings, two feet high.

Meeting the keeper later on, I demanded to know how the Forestry Commission could obstruct a sett like that. He merely grinned and said, 'Well, ask old badger if he minds!'

'But you're supposed to be taking care of the wildlife.'

'We had to take out about a dozen conifers that got cracked off in the Great Storm, you see, and that would have left the sett totally exposed, especially where it's so near the path, so we left all the brash to protect it, and the little new trees.'

I felt foolish and to make amends told him about the jammy bread.

'Reckon he's down deep now sleeping it off! There's a big old boar in there too, settled in for the winter I dare say,' the keeper said.

Hours of watching then, when the rutt was over. But a cold bright day promised another clear night, when I could stay on the beech slope and watch the fallow by moonlight, the mating season surely at its peak. When I returned to the wood that afternoon, entering quietly, slipping from tree to tree and eventually reaching my favourite fallen trunk, there was not a deer to be seen. Perhaps someone with dogs had just passed by? After an hour I was growing cold and stiff, so climbed back up to the path to warm up, catching a glimpse of movement down the next ride. A coal tit, small as a falling beech leaf, flew across my face; the whole wood smelled of autumn, earthy and fungoid. Across the grass ride a huge sweet chestnut had fallen in the Great Storm: roots and crown had been lopped away, but the trunk left to deter riders from galloping their horses up and down and churning up the turf. There was just room to walk round either end. The rut must be a boring time for young deer, still tied to their mothers but without their attention, doomed to stand about for hours watching the adults' antics with incurious eyes.

Half a dozen fawns had obviously got fed up with the whole thing, ganged together and gone off to play. Two or three were skittering up and down the ride, while one had jumped up onto the tree trunk. Framed by dark pines, he stood there, bright and cocky, four months grown, dark winter coat almost taken over, ears tall, head still with a trace of that blunt, puppy look of the very young, a tuft of grass hanging from his jaws, King of the Castle, till another, slightly smaller, jumped up beside him. They turned to stare at each other, then lowered heads, set little foreheads together and had a shoving match. When a third fawn landed lightly beside them, they both lost balance with surprise and fell off, breaking at once into a gallop and disappearing far down the ride, then tearing back again full tilt, while several others were playing chase round and round the fallen trunk.

Deep in the woods sounded a harsh cough, but, oblivious, two more fawns stole out from the conifers, stood and watched the gambolling for a moment. Presently one of them, still in summer dapple, ran forward and leapt clean over the trunk. The three nearest fawns froze as if playing statues. Dapples jumped lightly back, sailing through the darkening air in an elegant arc, with feet to spare. Another and another joined in this new game until the twilight was full of flying little bodies and a tawny owl flew off her day roost with a startled 'keewick keewick!'

By now a huge full moon had risen, covering the beech slope with a cold white light barred with black tree shadows. Does grazed here and there, eyes shining green-yellow when they looked up. A chill quiet pervaded the forest, birds gone to roost, not a squirrel stirring, even the owl mousing elsewhere, the only movement a solitary falling leaf. Once a small bird cheeped in its sleep. No moonlight could penetrate the thick needle canopy of the pines, it was a world of darkness. Night air lay on my face like a cold mask, and the sky glittered with stars. A twig cracked. The nearest doe sat down to chew her cud. Silence returned. In the shadows, bracket fungus gleamed, livid and magical.

Without so much as a warning rustle, a doe raced out of the pines below and away up the slope, King Buck galloping after, belching and roaring, with another doe chasing him; his great curved antlers shining in the moonlight. I ran uphill trying to glimpse them again through the silvery beech trunks. They seemed to be circling, perhaps back to the pines. In the excitement, I forgot all about keeping under cover. Why was a doe chasing the buck? Then they were right above, charging straight down towards me, the buck at full tilt, eyes bulging, mouth roaring, huge antlered. I dived behind the nearest tree, a four-foot hawthorn, feeling the wind of his passing, but of course his mind was not on me. Soon the leading doe, King Buck and the chasing doe had vanished back into the secret darkness of the pine wood. I longed to follow, but felt I should never be closer to the rut than the last few moments! I had never seen a doe chasing a buck before. The moon swung high above the beech trees and the forest fell back into shadowy silence.

Though some of the younger bucks might seize a last chance, as the moon waned over the next week, the forest would now calm down. A great gaunt buck shambled past Acorn Cottage, head low, ribs showing, the long fast over. It seemed a good time to revisit some old haunts before the year ended.

On Goose Lake not a single goose remained. Under a grey sky the pool stretched away, a dull pewter, to wooded banks faded as old tapestry, its only inhabitants a noisy raft of squabbling blackheaded gulls out in the middle. Then, as the eye grew attuned to all these muted colours, old acquaintances reappeared: in the western reach the great crested grebes still swam together as a pair, and out from a willow cove glided a whole flotilla of mallard. Under the pines opposite a solitary heron was fishing, a grey streak against dark trunks. A few rooks eddied about the sky, still in possession of the eastern pines, and, down among the dying parchment reeds, a moorhen pottered about.

Then over the raucous gulls sounded a high, mewing cry, and there black against the clouds circled a buzzard. There were no chicks at risk now, so the heron fished on, still as a rock. The rooks took no notice at first, then two peeled off and mobbed the predator in a half-hearted sort of way. The buzzard ignored them, hovering high over the reed bed, head down, intent on some movement down there, maybe the moorhen. But the reeds were still quite tall cover, he did not fancy landing among them and at last sailed away northward.

As dusk fell in the woods above, a white doe and her sandy fawn stepped delicately through the Castle gateway, paused a moment on a carpet of larch needles, then came in for the night, while on the common above, the scream of a hunting vixen, urgent and eerie, tore the darkening air. She was not after rabbits tonight, but a mate.

In the high forest at the source of Buckland Water, would the roe be playing at rutting – would they still be there at all?

Great toppling pinnacles of grey cloud with livid white edges sailed fast across a pale blue sky, a wild, windy, showery day. When cloud covered the sun, huge squalls blew up. A high wind roared through the tall beeches all the time shaking down the last coppery leaves in a constant shower, but this was nothing. Halfway down the slope a squall came up, howling and thundering through the trees; with a loud crack a bough was wrenched off, and fell somewhere quite close. I had to hang on to a trunk not to be blown flat; at least there was no need to tiptoe! Deer would not mind the wind, but they do tend, sensibly, to shelter from heavy rain so I made for the plantation of close young trees.

As I reached the top, another squall hurled across the wood from the south-west, this time bearing fat blobs of rain, so I took shelter on the north-east side of a wide oak, huddling between its root arms. What with the pelting rain, swirling leaves and roar of gale, I did not at first notice the little creature pottering through the slim beech poles, apparently oblivious of the storm.

The spot was just where I had seen the roe kids; but surely this was too small for even a half-grown roe? Peering through the rain, I realized it was one of my friendly hares, having a snack of moss. Small whirlwinds sucked up the leaves, spun them away, then tossed them down again, covering any droppings, hoofprints or scrapes, so it was no use searching for clues. Even that favourite tree stump where the roe used to play Chase-me-Charlie was all silted up with leaves.

Flailing branches revealed a glimpse of red brown out on the marshy flats; too red for winter roe, and anyway they never seemed to graze out there, grass coming a poor second best after browse. Presently a chorus of mooing announced that it was merely cattle. Best to go home then, return when it was quieter. I climbed up the steep bank between the beeches, was almost at the top, paused for breath in the buffeting wind, looked back. Small, brown-gold deer were running through the valley bottom along the line of fallen trees – a roe doe with a buck chasing her, tossing his handsome little antlers, galloping full pelt and both flying effortlessly over the clutter of dead branches and away up out of sight through the young beeches, but not before I had this last picture of them for the year, full of gaiety and glee.

The books were right about this then: roe did play mating games when the other deer were rutting, even though they had had their proper courting rites in May or June. The fertilized egg would only recently have implanted itself and pregnancy proper begun; does this trigger the play-chases? I would have waited a long time to see if they circled back, but when the ground shook with the crash of a falling tree, it seemed time to go home, leaving Swines Wood to its proper denizens.

A calmer atmosphere prevailed among the pines of Fenny Cross: on a still, misty day the sika hinds glanced up with mild interest as I crossed the bottom of their ride, soon going back to grazing with their calves. Down by the willowherb bank, a stretch of bare black mud betrayed a stag wallow, recently used. Hoof marks led away out of the woods, north-eastward. The rut could hardly be over when stags had been seen to mate as late as January, but as dusk fell, no banshee cries rent the air. Once more the Fenny Cross stags seemed to have vanished away.

Just at this time I received an unexpected present, a deer call. It was an elegantly finished double cylinder of polished walnut, resembling a pepper mill. Which kind of deer was it for? Blowing into the narrow end had no effect at all, but the wide end produced an astonishing noise like a very rude 'raspberry' or those things people blow and elongate at parties – a most un-deerlike sound. It drove George mad. Belatedly reading the instructions I discovered it was intended primarily for white-tailed deer, so was presumably American, but 'would call others'. Breathe into the mouthpiece so as to give a bleating effect and deer would come running from far and near! Such an effect was quite difficult to produce: light blowing produced silence, anything heavier, something raucous and rude. Eventually I could produce a passable bleat, though it was nothing like the tender little sound I had heard a doe utter on rutting night. I did not want to waste time blowing calls in an empty wood, or maybe frightening away other animals that were there already. Kings Ash would be the place. There were always fallow about there, so one would be able to see at once if the call had any effect, good or bad.

George usually came on winter walks, but I could not risk his howls being added to my bleats, so he had to stay on watch on the car glove shelf. Under a grey November sky, the great oaks and beeches, almost leafless now, spread away into far, dim glades, silent, secret, apparently deserted, but after I have leaned against an oak for a while, a squirrel skitters round the nearest tree and urgently buries an acorn, its coat the exact silver grey of beech bark, with a thin copper streak the colour of fallen leaves on the forest floor. Overhead a nuthatch is tapping away and a wren flies across my feet with a startled 'tick-tick'. In the wide clearings bracken still stands tall, good deer cover, even if its fronds are dried and a shining bronze in the misty air. Just here, one November, George had walked into the herd of red deer, but today there was not so much as a hoofprint. Was it worth trying out the call?

A scuttering of dead leaves made me look over to the right: it was of course a blackbird fussing about, but behind him deep in the fern I caught a flick of pale ear. It was worth a try. So the hushed air beneath the ancient trees is rent with a rude blast. Instantly, four heads shoot above the bracken, ears tall, dark shining eyes alert. Another bleat produces general movement, a bobbing head; three fallow does and two fawns walk out into the open to stare, from ten yards away. The fourth doe takes a little longer and when she joins them, I can see why. It is Hoofer, she of the slipper-sized hoof: it was her three-legged walk that caused that head-bobbing motion in the fern.

Game and gallant Hoofer! Foolishly I wanted to greet her. More rustling and out ran another fawn, five months grown with so dark a coat he must have been sired by a black buck, perhaps that very one I had tried to follow from Acorn Cottage, for there are not that many black bucks in the forest. He ran straight up to Hoofer and she turned, gave his left ear a brief lick over – Hoofer not only alive and well but with a perky young one!

They stood grouped together, staring at me. Another call would surely bring them closer, yet it seemed an intrusion on their world; I always felt something of an intruder among them, anyway. Fingering the smooth walnut of the whistle did conjure all sorts of images for the future, charming fallow does into the Castle, waking those dozy reds, finding the sika stags' summer hideaway . . .

But the whistle went back in my pocket. Could any watcher want more than this: a tawny owl's first cry of the evening, a last falling leaf of autumn, and Hoofer with her fawn vanishing away into the darkening winter woods?